CONVERSATION

CONVERSATIONS WITH BECKFORD

Memoirs of William Beckford from the *New Monthly Magazine* 1844

EDITED BY JON MILLINGTON

THE BECKFORD SOCIETY
2014

Published by The Beckford Society
The Timber Cottage, Crockerton, Warminster BA12 8AX

Printed and bound in Great Britain
by Berforts Information Press, Oxford

ISBN 978-0-9537836-6-3

INTRODUCTION

After William Beckford's death on 2 May 1844, the *New Monthly Magazine* lost no time in publishing a series of seven articles on him in the ensuing months. Cyrus Redding wrote the first three, and they appeared in June, July and August. It was understandable that he should have been chosen, because he had known Beckford for nine years and was later his first biographer. Beckford had wanted to met him after reading his very favourable review of the newly-published *Italy; with Sketches of Spain and Portugal* in the *Bath Guardian* for 12 July 1834: 'This work is from the pen of our accomplished fellow citizen, Mr Beckford who has long been distinguished in the world of letters, if not by the quantity of his productions, by the far more important adjunct of their high quality…'.

William Smith, Beckford's London printseller, chanced to hear him comment, 'Good heaven, here is one man that really understands me. He has caught the very best parts of my Italy, and I would give the world to know who he is. Can you find out for me? It is really a good work, though of my own production, but I don't think the fools of the present day are able to appreciate it. This man's criticism gives me a better idea of modern literature. As Pope said of Dr. Johnson, no matter who he is, he will soon be déterré'.[1]

As it happened, Beckford found out by other means that the reviewer was Cyrus Redding, editor of the weekly *Bath Guardian* since its inception in the February of that year, 1834. When he later asked to see the Tower on Lansdown, Beckford sent his carriage for him, and so began a friendship which lasted until Beckford's death.

Cyrus Redding was born at Falmouth in 1785, the son of a Baptist minister. At the age of twenty-one, he settled briefly in London and began work as a journalist. After returning to the West Country in

1808, he spent the years 1815–1818 in Paris as editor of *Galignani's Messenger.* From 1821 to 1830, he was the working editor and a major contributor to the *New Monthly Magazine* which was nominally edited by Thomas Campbell.[2] He followed this by two years as editor of another literary monthly, the *Metropolitan,* which failed in 1833, the year when his best-known book, *A History and Description of Modern Wines,* was published, using information acquired while he was in France. For a time he turned to provincial journalism, as first editor of the *Bath Guardian* until 1835, when he was persuaded to set up and edit another new paper, the *Staffordshire Examiner,* which he did for the next five years.

For the rest of his life Redding mainly devoted his energies to writing anecdotal books about the notable people he had met during his journalistic career. The autobiographical *Fifty Years' Recollections* of 1858 was the most successful and went into three editions in his lifetime. When he died in 1870 at the age of 86, the *Illustrated London News* was one of the periodicals carrying an obituary of him. Another was *Notes and Queries* which observed, 'It is not surprising that in later years this industrious writer and ready conversationalist, outliving his contemporaries, should have moved in a small circle, but the name of Cyrus Redding will not be forgotten as one of the hard labourers in the annals of literature.'[3]

This was the man who was one of the elderly Beckford's few visitors, and his rambling biography and other reminiscences, repetitive and even contradictory though they are, remain indispensable sources of information. Over a period of more than twenty years, Cyrus Redding wrote about Beckford on four occasions, the first being the two-part 'Recollections of the Author of "Vathek." ' in the *New Monthly Magazine*[4] reproduced here.

More than a decade later he followed this with a chapter on Beckford in *Fifty Years' Recollections.*[5] He repeated some of the anecdotes from the *New Monthly,* but there was also fresh material, including references to two books of his in Beckford's library. These were the *History of Wines* and *Gabrielle,* an early poem of 1829 about the Swiss Alps[6] which Redding presented to Beckford a few days before leaving Bath in 1835, bringing forth the acknowledgement, 'Mr Beckford will feel much pleasure in looking over this fervid and most impressive little poem with its author, any morning (between twelve and two) that might happen to suit Mr Redding's convenience.' When Redding came, Beckford went over the poem, which had been praised by Campbell and Rogers, and urged him to reissue it for the benefit of a wider public.[7]

Beckford's admiration of some, at least, of Redding's work makes it all the more surprising that none is to be found in the catalogue of the Beckford Library Sale of 1882–1883. Perhaps it was disposed of before the sale or withheld.

Fifty Years' Recollections was published amidst muted acclaim from such venerable monthlies as the *Gentleman's Magazine*. Their seven-page review ended with some extracts on Beckford, and this observation, 'The most interesting portion of Mr Redding's third volume is that occupied by his anecdotes of Beckford. He had good opportunities of becoming acquainted with this eccentric Croesus.'[8] His two-volume *Memoirs of William Beckford of Fonthill, Author of "Vathek."*[9] eventually appeared in the following year, having been suppressed in 1846 by Beckford's daughter, the Duchess of Hamilton. Boyd Alexander thought that she 'took strong exception to it for its revelation of her father's character.'[10]

Presumably Charles Skeet, publisher of both *Fifty Years' Recollections* and *Memoirs of William Beckford*, asked Redding for yet another book of anecdotes, and *Past Celebrities whom I Have Known* was the result. It contained fifty-five pages of by now familiar reminiscences of Beckford.[11]

Although Cyrus Redding's two-part 'Recollections' for the *New Monthly Magazine* are the liveliest of all his later pieces on Beckford, they are not chronological, as might be expected in an obituary. The first was accompanied by Freeman's round stipple engraving after the portrait of Beckford, now lost, by Piat Sauvage, previously engraved for the *European Magazine* of September 1797. These 'Recollections' were followed by 'The Tower of the Caliph' signed by Nerke, but Redding subsequently acknowledged his authorship in *Fifty Years'*

Recollections.[12] This article was written as if by a trespasser to Beckford's Tower, and Redding reprinted it almost verbatim in his *Memoirs of William Beckford*.[13]

In the next volume of the *New Monthly Magazine* were four further articles, though not by Cyrus Redding, being in a different style. Under the title 'Conversations with the late W. Beckford, Esq.', they were numbered III, IV, V and VI. Numbers III (signed H), IV and V form a continuous account and are undoubtedly by the same author who, from internal evidence, was an artist in his twenties living within an hour's drive from Bath with his father.[14] The artist had a sister who also met Beckford. Conversation No. VI was signed W.H.H. This was William Henry Harrison (1795?–1878), author of *Jennings' Landscape Annual or Tourist in Portugal*, 1839 (indirectly mentioned in the 'Conversation'), a work Beckford had in his library.[15] Additional evidence of the authorship of No. VI occurred when Harrison said he gave Beckford a short satire of his on Queen Victoria's visit to the City of London. This poem, published by Jennings in 1837, was *A Royal Dream of the Ninth of November* by the Wooden Spoon, known to be a pseudonym of Harrison's.

Guy Chapman, in the introductory Memoir to his edition of the *Travel-Diaries*, said of the contributors: 'All three obviously stood in terror of their host'.[16] Nevertheless, their recollections have an immediacy that was seldom matched, and the author of Conversations III-V went so far as to say that Beckford 'had taken absolutely possession of my faculties; in fact he haunted me; there was something so fascinating in his manner, and so amusing in his conversation–such a commingling of all that was impressive, affable, and kind, that, to use one of his own expressions, "I at once believed in him".'[17]

These seven articles were admirably complemented by Henry Venn Lansdown's four long letters describing the contents of Beckford's Tower and Lansdown Crescent. They were written to his sister in 1838 (with a fifth letter about his visit to Fonthill Abbey in 1844), but not published until some fifty years later by his daughter.[18] During the last five years of Beckford's life, Lansdown got to know him well, and later executed watercolours of his tower and tomb, and Fonthill Abbey. He also wrote a tribute to Beckford which appeared in the *Bath Herald.*[19]

An index of names at the end shows the range of artists, politicians and other notable people mentioned in the seven articles. Most have been identified, although a few remain a mystery. In some cases it proved difficult to establish which of several individuals with the same name was meant, but where possible the most likely one was chosen. Modern spelling of names appear in the index where they differ only slightly from those in the conversations.

1 Cyrus Redding, *Fifty Years' Recollections, Literary and Personal, With Observations on Men and Things.* London: C. J. Skeet, 1858. 3 vols. Vol. 3, p. 120.
2 Samuel Carter Hall, *Retrospect of a Long Life from 1815 to 1883.* London: Bentley, 1883. 2 vols. Vol. 1, p. 315.
3 *Notes and Queries*, 4th Series, vol. 5 (4 June 1870): 550.
4 *New Monthly Magazine and Humorist* 71 (June, July 1844): 143–158, 302–319.
5 *Fifty Years' Recollections.*, vol. 3, pp. 87–124.
6 For a discussion about *Gabrielle*, see Jerry Nolan, 'Redding's Alps and Beckford's Pencillings', *Beckford Journal* 10 (2004): 61–70.
7 *Fifty Years' Recollections*, vol. 3, pp. 92 and 106.
8 *Gentleman's Magazine* 204 (May 1858): 494.
9 *Memoirs of William Beckford of Fonthill. Author of "Vathek."*, London: C. J. Skeet, 1859. 2 vols. 352, 402 pp.
10 Boyd Alexander, *England's Wealthiest Son.* London: Centaur, 1962. p. 4.
11 *Past Celebrities whom I Have Known.* London: C. J. Skeet, 1866. Vol. 1, pp. 292–347.
12 *Fifty Years' Recollections*, vol. 3, p. 87.
13 *Memoirs of William Beckford*, vol. 2, pp. 261–278.
14 For a study of this young artist's encounters with Beckford, see Jerry Nolan, "Beckford in Bath According to 'H'", *Beckford Journal* 13 (2007): 54–66.
15 Sotheby, *Catalogue of the Second Portion of the Beckford Library removed from Hamilton Palace,* 1882, Lot 574.

16 Guy Chapman, ed., *The Travel-Diaries of William Beckford of Fonthill,* London: Constable, 1928. Vol. 1, p. lv, note 1.

17 *New Monthly Magazine and Humorist* 72 (Sept 1844): 19. There were no further articles in 1845.

18 *Recollections of the Late William Beckford of Fonthill, Wilts and Lansdown, Bath.* Bath: Privately printed, 1893. Facsimile reprint, Bath: Kingsmead, [1969].

19 *Bath Herald,* 18 May 1844, 3e. Also, with omissions, in *The Times,* 23 May 1844, 6a.

THE

NEW MONTHLY MAGAZINE

AND

HUMORIST.

CONTENTS FOR JUNE.

CONTENTS FOR JULY.

CONTENTS FOR AUGUST.

CONTENTS FOR SEPTEMBER.

CONTENTS FOR OCTOBER.

CONTENTS FOR NOVEMBER.

CONTENTS FOR DECEMBER.

William Beckford Esqre

THE

NEW MONTHLY MAGAZINE

AND

Humorist.

1844.

PART THE SECOND.

LONDON:
HENRY COLBURN, GREAT MARLBOROUGH ST.
SOLD BY ALL BOOKSELLERS.

C. WHITING, BEAUFORT HOUSE, STRAND.

THE

NEW MONTHLY MAGAZINE.

RECOLLECTIONS OF THE AUTHOR OF "VATHEK."

BY CYRUS REDDING, ESQ.

The "Author of Vathek" is no more. Another of the writers left to us who had attained a lasting reputation in English literature, to quote his own expression on the death of the archbishop-confessor of Portugal, "has been summoned to the presence of Him, before whom no flesh living shall be justified." His literary career was protracted—no less than fifty-eight years elapsing between the appearance of the "Memoirs of Extraordinary Painters," and the "Visit to Alcobaça." His mind was vigorous, his spirits were good, and he displayed his wonted activity of body nearly to the last. He declared to the present writer, in his seventy-sixth year, that he never felt a minute's *ennui* in his life. To this the great variety of his mental resources, as well as his bodily temperament, which would never permit him to remain inactive, greatly contributed. He was the most accomplished man of his time; his reading was perhaps the most extensive. Besides the classical languages of antiquity, he spoke five modern European tongues, writing three of them with great elegance. He read the Persian and Arabic, was an excellent designer with the pencil, and a perfect master of the science of music. The last he was taught by Mozart, to whom he was so attached, that when the great musician settled in Vienna, he made a visit to that capital, as he said himself, "that he might once more see his old master."

Coming early into the possession of a large fortune, and considerable landed property, both in England and Jamaica—of which latter island, his great-great-grandfather had been lieutenant-governor and commander of the forces, and his grandfather, president of the council—he did not neglect the cultivation of his literary taste. Lords Chatham and Camden, the friends of his father, the celebrated chief magistrate of London, were consulted upon the subject of his education. His acquirements show that their advice was not neglected; his sublime tale of "Vathek" written in early life was proof of this. His splendid buildings at Fonthill long attracted public attention from their cost and magnitude. There was the *prestige* of vastness about all his conceptions. When he sold and quitted Fonthill, he was scarcely known to be in Bath, before a beautiful tower, planned in the purest taste, suddenly appeared on the summit of the highest eminence in the vicinity. Half an extensive hillside was enclosed.

Massy stone portals uprose here and there as if by magic, their creation being the employment of his leisure hours to superintend. He thus expended large sums with mechanics and work-people, while he preserved his health by devoting a portion of his time to employment in the open air; this he considered an essential to a sanatory existence.

I became acquainted with the "Author of Vathek," about nine years before his decease, being at the time resident temporarily in Bath. When about to leave that place, I felt desirous to enter the tower so conspicuous upon Lansdown. Fonthill, with its departed magnificence, naturally awakened my curiosity in regard to the new edifice. About the same time, the "Sketches" of Italy, Spain, and Portugal, appeared together with a new French edition of the most sublime and powerfully written tale of any English author, the long far-famed "Vathek."

Leading his life of accustomed seclusion, the "Author of Vathek" was only known in Bath as the mysterious haughty gentleman who lived in Lansdown Crescent. Some there were who thought he passed his time in working incantations, like his own Caliph. Surmises were current about a brood of dwarfs that vegetated in an apartment built over the archway connecting his two houses. The vulgar, poor and rich alike, gave a sort of half credit to cabalistical monstrosities invoked in that apartment. In a place of fashionable dissipation, picture-galleries, a noble library, fine gardens, and the resources of intellect, to say nothing of a large domain of hillside, were no accountable means of passing time without a participation in the reigning frivolities of the hour; astrology, and the supernatural vocation of the Giaour, were indispensable to make up the imaginary deficiency. The *per contra* arguments were the presence of the "Author of Vathek" at the floral shows in the city and vicinity before the crowd attended, his intercourse with a few intellectual and professional men, and his being sometimes seen riding through the streets on a cream-coloured Arabian, in place of the mystical Alborac of the prophet—not unfrequently in company with the Duke of Hamilton.

In the west-end of London, the "Author of Vathek," was better known than in Bath, at such times as he visited his house in Park-lane. He might then be seen calling of a morning upon a few old friends; entering a bookseller's shop—for with "the trade" he dealt largely; or talking, in his depository of pictures for sale, to some respectable dealer. Every one who trafficked in first-rate paintings knew him well. They have assured me that they never offered him any fine work of art, of which he could not tell them the exact value. Sometimes they tendered him a rarity for no other purpose than to ascertain its real worth. If he offered a price for a picture he never gave more, but if the offer were declined, he uniformly abandoned the purchase. If what he sought to purchase were really good, he was not niggardly in his tender, though the sum was his ultimatum.

A friend of mine has seen him, after he turned his eighty-second year, ride through Hyde Park, along the Edgware-road, as far as West End, pull up his horse near that rural spot opposite the entrance to what was once his father's villa, and appear lost in thought—in association, perhaps, with bygone years. Farther on, half way up the hill to Hampstead, he was more than once observed, a year or two ago, to stop and gaze over the far-spread landscape beneath, at the hues of sunset, perhaps recalling the lines of Dante which he told me he had often quoted on the same occasion in the southern countries of Europe, beginning "Era gia l'ora," and concluding with the beautiful reference to the village chimes in Catholic lands—

Che paja 'l giorno pianger, che si muore.

Equally strangers with those who gossiped at the York House, or others who so shrewdly conjectured the existence of a dwarfish Abracadabra in the city of Bladud, as to the eccentricities of the "Author of Vathek," and being about to leave the place, I had naturally a wish to see the tower. The ingenious architect employed in its erection, was the individual to whom I applied for that object. He informed me that he once had permission to issue tickets for the purpose himself, but for reasons which he felt to be perfectly satisfactory, the permission had been withdrawn:—still he had only to ask for a ticket, and he should receive it as a matter of course.

In a day or two after I had thus expressed my wish, I received, not without considerable surprise, a note from the architect, to the following purport:

"Mr. Beckford has given directions for his carriage to convey you to Lansdown Tower. Afterwards, he himself will show you his house and paintings. If you will apprise me by letter whether Monday or Tuesday will suit I will arrange accordingly."

I resided at Lincombe, on the southern side of the city; Lansdown is upon the northern. The tower stands upon the summit, so far back from the brow of the hill, that it cannot be seen from the streets, which are too immediately under the height—an elevation of eight hundred feet. It was not more than a couple of miles from my residence—an easy walk. The tender of the carriage was therefore as unexpected and unaccountable, as civility of any kind from one who lived so retired, and who was deemed the most reserved man in England—total stranger as I was. No matter; I accepted the offer with a suitable acknowledgment, fixing the time as I was requested to do. An elegant, yellow-bodied chariot drove to my door. I passed through the city to Lansdown by Milsom-street and York Buildings. Some who saw me were as much at a loss to account for my appearance in the equipage as I was myself. It became a wonder—a conjecture—unsolvable during that day among the gossips.

On reaching the entrance to the grounds on the left-hand side upon the hill summit, I found that not the potent influence of Carathis with her enchantments, could have procured me a more facile entrance to the tower of the Caliph, than I found here—to a site barred and banned as report gave out, to the general curiosity. I sent home the carriage and servants, that I might walk to the Crescent through the private grounds. The outer gate closed upon me. I approached the handsome structure erected by the imaginative Author of "Vathek"—by him who had constructed a far more enduring edifice, the product of unperishable genius:—

"Before that work the iron and stone tower vanish—time will leave no wreck of *them*," thought I; "though time may possess the talisman that gives ruin entrance here, the tower of the Caliph carries the enduring stamp of immortality."

At the door I found domestics ready to answer every question. The architect joined me as I entered the structure which was the talk of every body, and is really so ornamental an object. Many denominated it a foolish thing, for the foremost of all reasons of authority with John Bull—that the money might have been laid out to more profit!

I found the cabinets unlocked, the book-cases flung wide open, the mysteries of the beautiful tower displayed as freely for my inspection as if the costly objects had been my own property. There were two or three rooms filled with books, and articles of *virtù* arranged with the utmost taste. Vases, busts, statues, rich porcelain, exquisite paintings, too, were disposed with sober judgment—nothing was overdone. In the angles of the two principal rooms elegant vessels of China or crystal, were placed with bouquets of freshly-gathered flowers, imparting delicious fragrance around—a thing with which Mr. Beckford never dispensed, while flowers were procurable. I examined several of the books which were the better editions of the ancient classics, with the best French, Italian, and English authors, These were designed for use should the owner feel inclined to remain and breakfast after an early morning visit to the hill. There were a kitchen beneath and pantries with every convenience for a *déjeuner* or *refresco*. One long, narrow room was fitted up as an oratory. It was lit by small domes in the roof, which the architect had so contrived as to throw down a soft, subdued, harmonious light, upon marble figures of the Virgin and Child at the end, opposite the entrance. The repose which reigned in the room, through the soothing effect of the light, was peculiarly impressive.

"That is the true light of devotion," Mr. Beckford afterwards observed to me. "It is an excitement in itself to solemn thoughts and prayer—the dim religious light of the sanctuary. It was that light which they intended to pervade the old cathedrals. The Bath abbey-church is of the later Gothic—too light for such an effect."

The property in the tower was worth from twenty to thirty thousand pounds. I heard subsequently, that three or four years afterwards this property was removed, with the view of furnishing the tower in a plainer manner. There was one piece of *verd antique* supporting a vase of flowers, worth at least a thousand pounds. An attempt had been made to break into this charming retreat during the night. Though great efforts were exerted, the strength of the workmanship resisted the thieves so long, that they were forced to decamp without attaining their end. The intelligence was communicated to Mr. Beckford by the architect, who was somewhat flurried as he gave the information. The observation in reply was characteristic of the owner, who early in the morning was flinging bread to a brood of turkeys at the back of his house.

"The tower has been broken into by thieves, sir."

"Have they carried off any thing—is much injury done?" inquired Mr. Beckford, calmly.

"There is nothing gone," was the reply, "but they have done great injury to the building—they very nearly attained their object."

"Mr. G——, Mr. G——, do not be so excited—don't show so much

emotion. Where will you, and I, and the tower be in a few years? A hundred pounds will set all right again, I dare say—don't be excited."

We ascended to the room at the top of the tower. This room is within the lantern. The last is principally of cast iron, copied from the Choragic monument of Lysicrates at Athens, resting upon a square base formed by the walls of the tower. The tower up to the lantern gracefully diminishes from the foundation; it is about a hundred and thirty feet high.

The appearance of hill-top after hill-top on the Somersetshire side of the Avon, unmasked to the eye during the ascent, had a novel and beautiful effect. On every side the view was striking. All the southern shore of the Avon, opposite Bath, was visible. In the north-west direction, the sight, after ranging over the barren table-land of the down, unadorned with a single tree, was arrested by the solitary monument of Sir Beville Granville, who fell in the battle of Lansdown. The view naturally tinctured with melancholy, was still more saddened by the monument and its associations.

The tower of Fonthill Abbey was visible from thence before it fell. Mr. Beckford was the only individual who could see it was no more in the field of view without a telescope. He missed his former property, the day after it fell, before the news had reached Bath.

At seventy-five his activity was so great, he could mount rapidly to the top of the tower without halting—no small exertion for many who were fifteen or twenty years younger. The windows in the lantern were of plate-glass, moving in perpendicular grooves. The wind at that elevation being exceedingly violent, great strength of material was required. The curtains of the room were crimson. Warm air from below was conveyed by heated tubes to the lantern, that the damp might not be injurious to the woodwork.

I descended, and passed out of the tower into a shrubbery, kept with strict adherence to the wildness of nature. No trim walks—no nicely-edged borders were there, the paths being such only as were worn by the passengers' feet. Choice flowers grew amid heaps of stone, from which they appeared to spring naturally. The aspect being warm, and the spot sheltered, many plants flourished well there that would scarcely vegetate upon another site. I noticed a small marble monument, designed for the place of interment of a favourite dog. The animal, from its advanced age, was thought to be nearly approaching its end; it had been remarkably fond of the master who thus anticipated a memorial of its burying-place.

My guide through the shrubbery and to the house, as I descended Lansdown, was Mr. Beckford's gardener, a few years younger than his master. He had planted Fonthill. The hedges were not clipped, nor the parterres laid out in fantastic figures. He told me that his master overlooked every operation himself—there was not a plant or flower there with which he was unacquainted. I entered, on leaving the shrubbery, a garden, the surface of which was sunk far beneath the surrounding level, parallel with the high road, from which it was separated by a lofty wall. This garden was judiciously formed in an ancient stone quarry. Every tree and plant flourished there luxuriantly. From this garden I emerged upon the turf (since planted), and continuing to descend, was at last stopped by a massy portal, resembling the entrance to the castle of some giant Blue-beard. Having gone through this I came into a second garden filled with fruit-trees. Nectarines and peaches strewed the walks—the year having been a plentiful one of fruit. Crossing this second garden, I found myself close to the arch which Mr. Beckford had built for connecting two houses, and in a few moments I was at the door of his mansion in Lansdown Crescent. It cannot be supposed I was destitute of curiosity to discover the cause of the attention with which I had been so honoured, nor a whit less curious to have an interview with the "Author of Vathek"—one of whom the world had spoken so much and knew so little.

My attendants escorted me to the door, knocked and went their way. It was opened by the porter, who was a dwarf, apparently middle-aged, stout, but not remarkably short for one of his race. The origin of the story about dwarf inhabitants of the mansion was thus cleared up. A second servant led the way up a spacious staircase to the drawing-room floor, announced my name, and retired. I observed that the staircase and landing-place were hung as thickly with fine paintings as they could be suspended. There was a full length of Mr. Beckford's father, who died in 1770, and the original portrait of himself, engraved and published in his account of Alcobaça and Batalha, both by Reynolds.

I saw in a moment that the arch from house to house was a continuation of the drawing-room floor, which extended it to nearly double the original size. The entire length was occupied as a library, and filled—literally crammed with books in fine condition. There was nothing showy, at the same time that every thing bore the impress of perfect good taste; the hangings, furniture, tables, all were handsome, nothing extravagant. The windows were of plate-glass; on the elegant library-tables were numerous handsome bound volumes. I walked towards the further end of the room, from whence Mr. Beckford, then in his seventy-fourth year, but in appearance some years younger, came to meet me. I bowed, he returned the salutation. I thanked him for the unexpected honour that I, a stranger, had received at his hands. He smiled, welcomed me with the affability and air of a finished gentleman of the old school, inquired how I liked the tower, whether I had examined the books, some of which were rare editions, and what I thought of it as a place of study. I replied that my time had been too short to look into more than one or two of the voluminous collection deposited there—that in those I did look at I saw his notes—that I was too anxious to avail myself of the invitation to his mansion, and a personal interview, to lose a moment in a secondary and distant object. I had noticed an edition of Wilkes's Letters, and some works belonging to the earlier years of the reign of George III., a period about which I had always felt a peculiar interest, as the prelude to the disposition of things that in subsequent years involved England in a succession of evils. Mr. Beckford replied that it was a period of great interest to himself on many accounts; he thought he had all the publications of that time.

In person he was scarcely above the middle height, slender, but well formed, with features indicating great intellectual power. His eyes were wonderfully acute, his apprehension exceedingly quick, his enunciation rather more rapid than that of the average of speakers in general. His constitution had not, according to his own account, been strong. In early life he had been unable in consequence to remain in parliament, though he had sat both for Wells and Hindon. By activity, temperance, and care, more than all by spending as much time as possible in the open air, with plenty of exercise, he had rendered himself comparatively hale. He was dressed in a green coat with cloth buttons, a buff striped waistcoat, breeches of the same kind of cloth as the coat, and brown topboots, the fine cotton stockings appearing over them, in the fashion of a gentleman thirty or forty years ago. I never saw him in any other costume when indoors. To return to my interview.

Upon again acknowledging my sense of the kindness so unexpectedly shown me, without being able to discover wherefore I had been so treated, Mr. Beckford replied that he knew my name well. "Though I see few persons, I know all that passes connected with literature or art," looking towards an ample table, upon which lay several periodical works. "There," he continued, pointing to a book-case, "is a volume of which you are the author. But I have engaged to be your Cicerone; do me the favour to sit, and I will show you some of the curious works in my possession."

I sat down, not without a desire to examine the treasures in the multitudinous collection around me; a vain wish that it would have taken long to gratify: upon the Spanish and Portuguese chronicles alone I could have bestowed a month. Mr. Beckford set before me an eastern MS., the substance of which appeared to be a species of leather. It had once belonged to Shah Aulum, at Delhi. There were painted upon it what seemed to be portrait resemblances of the great men of the Mogul empire, with various ceremonies. The lines in the execution of these portraits could not have been retouched, and must therefore have required a practised hand and wonderful skill to delineate. Affable and easy in manner, in the way of the old school, the owner entered into explanations which have escaped my memory, from the small interest I took in a subject with which I was so little familiar. It was not so with my desire to examine the other works contained there, which I hope will be preserved in Hamilton Palace,—never dispersed.

"I am fond of the East," said Mr. Beckford.

I replied I should have thought as much from his tale of "Vathek." It was one of the works which had delighted me from my youth—the most striking and imaginative I ever read. Mr. Beckford seemed to forget he had volunteered to be Cicerone. Neither of us rose from our chairs to the book-cases. His conversation was exceedingly interesting. I lamented I knew nothing of Eastern literature, endeavouring to return to the subject of "Vathek."

"I thought of the Tower of the Caliph just now," I remarked, "while I was upon Lansdown, fancying the youthful idea carried on through later life—the towers in 'Vathek,' at Fonthill, and here, lead to such a conclusion."

"No," he replied, "I have extraordinary sight; God rarely gives men such eyes. I am partial to glancing over a wide horizon—it delights me to sweep far along an extended landscape. I must elevate myself to do this, even on Lansdown. The tower at Fonthill was as necessary an appendage to such a structure as it would have been to a real abbey. I love building, planting, gardening—whatever will keep me employed in the open air. I like to be among workmen. I never kept less at one time than a hundred when at Fonthill. Wishing to have something besides a study on the summit of the hill where the view is so extensive, I determined upon erecting the tower."

"It was a conclusion from the advantageous site then?" I observed.

"It was—every body is deceived in judging of the motives of others, though your conclusion was natural."

"The Tower of the Caliph is so prominent in 'Vathek' that I am not the only person who labours under the mistake. 'Vathek' made a great sensation when it appeared?" I continued, wishing to obtain all the information possible about a favourite book.

"You will hardly believe how closely I was able to apply myself to study when young. I wrote 'Vathek' when I was barely twenty-two years of age. I wrote it at one sitting, in French. It cost me three days and two nights of hard labour. I never took off my clothes the whole time. This severe application made me very ill."

"Your mind must have been ardent, and deeply imbued with the literature of the East?"

"I revelled day and night in that sort of reading for a good while—I preferred it to the classics, and began it as a relief from their dryness. I was a much better Latin than Greek scholar—the Greek and Latin were set tasks. I began Persian of my own accord."

"The 'Hall of Eblis,' Byron praises highly for its sublimity."

"Byron several times complimented me upon that story."

"I never read a description in the Eastern writings, through translation of course, that contains any thing like the 'Hall of Eblis,'" I observed.

"You could hardly find any thing like it there, for that was my own. Old Fonthill had a very ample, lofty, loud echoing hall, one of the largest in the kingdom. Numerous doors led from it into different parts of the house, through dim, winding passages. It was from that I introduced the hall—the idea of the 'Hall of Eblis' being generated by my own. My imagination magnified and coloured it with the Eastern character. All the females in 'Vathek' were portraits of those in the domestic establishment of old Fonthill, their fancied good or ill qualities exaggerated to suit my purpose."

"I have heard that Sir Walter Scott copied most of his characters and landscape descriptions from such as really existed," I remarked.

"I did something of the sort by accident in 'Vathek'—it was the impulse of my own mind—but I had to elevate, exaggerate, and orientalize every thing. I was soaring on the Arabian bird roc, among genii and enchantments, not moving among men. I have the French edition of 'Vathek' recently printed—pray accept a copy."

I thanked him, remarking that the 'Hall of Eblis' itself was equalled, in my view, if not surpassed by the sublime description of the descent thither—the rapidity of the steps, their continued acceleration until the sensation was that of falling from a precipice.

"I forget. Have the goodness to show me the passage," said Mr. Beckford.

I turned to it. "Comme ils se hâtaient avec une ardente impatience, leurs pas s'accélérèrent à un point qu'ils semblaient tomber rapidement dans un précipice, plutôt que marcher."

"It did not strike me before," said the author; "that the description is obscure, as it affects the cause of acceleration. There is sublimity in mystery, they say—it is not bad. Do you know Sir William Ouseley told me long ago that what I have called the "watch-towers" built upon the terrace of the palace of Istakar, were in reality columns now or recently in existence. A column would have been more appropriately consecrated to a star than a watch-tower."

I inquired whether the three episodes of "Vathek" were still in existence, remarking how strongly Byron had expressed his desire to see them —the histories of Alasi and Firouz, of Prince Barkiarokh, of Kalilah and Zulkais, who were shut up in the palace of subterranean fire.

He replied that he had destroyed one of these histories, because he thought it would be deemed too wild, but that the other two might some day see the light. I had written of "Vathek" as the author's first literary performance.

"You were wrong," said he, "in calling 'Vathek' my first literary production. You suppose also that I translated it from the French original. I wrote the 'Memoirs of Extraordinary Painters' before I wrote 'Vathek.' The translator of 'Vathek' I do not know—it was tolerably well done."

I here remarked that it missed some of the author's quaintnesses. The translator had rendered for example the passage "Bababalouk, who, in capacity of purveyor, had acquitted himself with applause, as to peacocks and turtles, lost no time in consigning some dozens to the spit." The translation should be "Bababalouk, who had not overlooked the fatness of the peacocks and turtle doves, lost no time," &c.

"There may be more instances of the same kind," replied Mr. Beckford, "but as a whole it has not done me injustice."

No sketch or plan of "Vathek" appears to have been made; it was struck off from the author's mind *currente calamo.* I never read the "Memoirs of Extraordinary Painters," I remarked.

"It is a laughable book. The editor of the *Quarterly Review* seems to have read it. He says he is 'not aware under what circumstances it was given to the world.' I will tell you how it originated. Do you know the editor of the *Quarterly?*"

I replied that I had a slight knowledge of him—I considered him one of the ablest of our living writers—a very accomplished man, though I did not pay the same compliment to some of his contributors, I deemed his novels superior to those of any other writer of the day. Mr. Beckford thought Mr. Lockhart's novels were not properly appreciated. "How should they," said he, "when little but rubbish is current? The *Quarterly* complimented me on this work, which I threw off as a sort of *jeu d'esprit.* It is true enough, as the reviewer states, that I designed to hit the criticisms and memoirs upon Dutch painters. How could I fail to do so with such an opportunity—their fooleries and trash so very obvious! I will explain the origin of the 'Memoirs.' The housekeeper at old Fonthill, as is customary, used to get her fee by exhibiting the pictures to those who came to see the building. Once or twice I overheard her give the most extraordinary names to different artists. I wondered how such nonsense could enter the brain of woman. More than this, in her conceit she would at times expatiate upon excellencies of which the picture before her had no trace. The temptation was irresistible, in my humour. I was but seventeen. My pen was quickly in hand composing the 'Memoirs.' In future the housekeeper had a printed guide in aid of her descriptions. She caught up my phrases; the fictitious names of the wives too, whom I had given to my imaginary painters, were soon learned in addition; her descriptions became more picturesque, her language more graphic than ever!"

"To the visiters of old Fonthill?"

"Yes, to the sight-seeing people. Mine was the text-book, whoever exhibited the paintings. The book was soon on the tongues of all the domestics. Many were the quotations current upon the merits of Og of Basan, and Watersouchy of Amsterdam. Before a picture of Rubens or Murillo there was often a charming dissertation upon the pencil of the Herr Sucrewasser of Vienna, or that great Italian artist Blunderbussiana, of Venice. I used to listen unobserved until I was ready to kill myself with laughing, at the authorities quoted to the squires and farmers of Wilts, who took all for gospel. It was the most ridiculous thing in effect that you can conceive. Between sixty and seventy years ago people did not know so much of the fine arts as they do now. Not but that they have much still to learn."

"There are excellent hits in the 'Memoirs,' according to the *Quarterly*," I observed; "but it required the result of observation and experience to satirize so keenly the follies of the Dutch biographers."

"Great pains had been bestowed upon my education. I was living amidst a fine collection of works of art, under competent tutors. I was studious and diligent from inclination. I was fond of reading whatever came in my way. After my classical studies were finished, and while I worked hard at Persian, I read French and English biography of all sorts."

"You visited France at an early age?"

"Before I was eighteen I had mingled in French society. I was introduced in Paris to Voltaire, who died the same year. On taking leave of him, he placed his hand upon my head, 'There, young Englishman,' said he, 'I give you the blessing of a very old man!' Voltaire was a mere skeleton—a living anatomy—his countenance I shall never forget. I travelled southward, and in the same year visited the Grande Chartreuse."

"There are some verses of yours in the Album there," I observed, "though not in the account of your visit recently published."*

---

* These verses are yet to be found in the Album of the fathers. Gray's celebrated lines, beginning "O tu, severi Religio loci," dated 1741, precede them but a little way.

Inscribed in the Album of the Grande Chartreuse.

To orisons the midnight bell
Had toll'd each silent inmate from his cell;
The hour was come to muse or pray,
Or work mysterious rites that shun the day!
My steps some whispering influence led
Up to yon pine-clad mountain's gloomy head.
Hollow and deep the gust did blow
And torrents dash into the vales below!
The summit high at length attain'd,
A moonlight chequer'd darkness round me reign'd,
As fearful to my searching eye
A shadowy form glanced near, then flitted by!
Anon before my face it stood—
A bearded figure, pale, in pensive mood—

"I had forgotten them. They are not very poetical, I suppose. There never was a finer field for poetry—a more striking scene. I have a vivid recollection of its grand solitudes. The brethren too were excellent people—not one now survives whom I saw—death has swept them all away."

I expressed my apprehension that I was trespassing upon his leisure. He assured me I was not, and then observed, "You wrote a criticism upon my 'Italy, Spain, and Portugal.' I knew it was yours. If you had read my thoughts—if you could have understood beforehand the springs that moved me in my observations, you could not have struck upon them more surely. I feel I am indebted to you for your remarks. The moment your wishes were made known to me about the tower, I requested my carriage might be offered you, with every facility I could afford for your gratification, as far as my means of satisfying your curiosity extended. My 'sketches' were drawn up from notes very inefficient in themselves; but my memory supplied what was wanting."

I thanked him, and reverting to the "Sketches in Italy," observed that I knew perfectly every minute object described in the first six chapters of the second volume.

"Then tell me," said he, "if you think the description faithful." I replied in the affirmative—that some objects were so accurately delineated, I was at home instantly in the scene of my boyhood. The stone pyramid, the scent of wall-flowers, the grove of tall elms, Arwenick,

---

Cold horror thrill'd me till it spoke
And accents faint the charm—held silence broke:—
"Long, traveller, ere this region near,
Say, did not whisperings strange arrest thine ear?
My summons they to bid thee come
Where sole the friend of nature loves to roam.
Seven ages past, this drear abode,
To solitude I sanctified and God!
'Twas here by love of wisdom brought,
Her truest lore self-knowledge first I sought:
Devoted here my worldly wealth,
To win my chosen sons immortal health!
Mid these black woods and mountains steep,
Mid the wild horrors of yon desert deep,
Mid yawning caverns, watery dells,
Mid long sequestered aisles and peaceful cells,
No passions fell distract the mind,
To silence, nature, and herself resigned.
In these still mansions who shall bide,
'Tis mine with Heaven's appointment to decide.
But hither I invite not all,
Some want the will to come and some the call—
But all, mark now my parting voice,
Led or by chance, necessity, or choice—
(Oh—with our genius fear to sport!)
Sage lessons here may learn of high import.
Know silence is the nurse of truth!—
Know temperance long retards the flight of youth!—
Learn hence how penitence and prayer,
Man's fallen race may happier worlds prepare!—
Show mild demeanour, void of art,
And bear amidst the world the Hermit-heart!
Farewell! may BRUNO's words prevail!"
He said, and sunk into the misty vale!

June 8, 1778. WILLIAM BECKFORD.

once the seat of the Killegrews—Trefusis—the vast brakes of furze scenting the air with the perfume of violets—the primroses and violets in bloom the first week in March—the soft blue sky, the calm sea, and the fishing-boats—his picture was familiar to me at once—"and more," I added, "you were walking to and fro frequently, before the very door where I was then a toddling infant."

"That is singular," said he; "and by accident, after more than half a century, we approximate again in Lansdown Crescent! Human destiny is a puzzle—how blind we are to the course of our coming existence. What are become of my Portuguese friends whom I was then going to see? Death has taken them all! There is that busy little despot Miguel —you know whose son he is?"

I replied in the negative.

"The reputed of young Don Pedro, Marquis of Marialva, whose father was my friend. Don Pedro, remarkable enough, was web-footed. You may have read and inferred something from a passage in my Alcobaça and Batalha, where I ran a race, at the desire of the Infanta, Princess of Brazil, with two of her maids of honour."

"Was the Portuguese court remarkably dissolute?"

"Not more so than other courts were at that time. There was great goodness of heart in some of the nobility and ecclesiastics; but they were an indolent, luxurious race. The country people were excellent, tainted with few vices; the character of the Lisbon *canaille* abominable—the most flagrant vices were common in the towns. The ignorance of all classes, too, was deplorable. The Prior of St. Vincent's, my friend, was an ecclesiastic of great learning and accomplishments—an excellent man. There were few his equals in Portugal. But the beauty of nature there—it was a heaven upon earth—I long more than ever for such a climate here."

I arose and took leave; the day was drawing rapidly on. Mr. Beckford came to the head of the staircase, pointing out the subjects of some of the paintings, as I, descending, wished him good morning. He requested that before I left Bath, I would call upon him, without ceremony, as often as I felt inclined—that he would always be at home to me between twelve and two.

His custom, in fine weather, was to rise early, ride to the tower, walk back and breakfast, and then read until a little before noon, generally making pencil notes in the margin of the book—transact business with his steward afterwards, until two o'clock continue to read or write, and then if the weather was fine, ride out for exercise. He was never idle. When planting or building, he passed the larger part of the day where the work was proceeding. A professional friend of mine found him out in his grounds alone one day, about a year ago, busily employed cutting up thistles. He sometimes expressed contempt by a sarcastic look peculiar to himself. Few could utter more cutting things than the author of "Vathek." The utterance was accompanied with a caustic expression of countenance that made them tell with double effect.

I did not fail to make use of the general invitation I had received. Upon my next call, I found the author of "Vathek" in a sitting-room on the entrance-floor of his house. He was seated at an upright grand piano, of remarkably fine tone. The instrument was placed at the further end of the room from the window, which faced the south against a curtain of fine scarlet cloth, hung very full along the wall, and suspended near the ceiling by rings to a bright metal rod. On inquiring the purpose of this curtain, Mr. Beckford told me that it was to prevent the wall behind from deflecting the sound of the instrument. He rose on my entrance, and before I had taken a seat, requested me to look at the St. Catherine of Raphael, hanging over the fire-place. This picture is now in the National Gallery.* Turning the key in the lock of the plate-glass frame placed before it for the sake of preservation, but from its reflection, injurious to a perfect view of the painting, he asked, "Is not that beautiful?"

I replied, I thought it very fine, but that Raphael seemed as partial to *embonpoint* in his females as Rubens was.

"No," said Mr. Beckford, "the women of Raphael are Italian in grace—they look round, firm, and well-formed; the ladies of Rubens are Flemish or Dutch, flaccid and oysterish, as if they had been fattened in their own quags or salt-marshes."

There were a number of fine pictures in this apartment, but their owner drew my attention to the St. Catherine alone, saying, he had attempted to write some verses upon it, and failed. He was too old to write poetry. I said it was an inspiring theme. "Try it," he replied.

"There has been a paragraph," he observed, as he drew his chair to the opposite side of the table, taking a seat by his book and pencil, his common companions indoors, *vis à vis* to where I sat. "There has been a paragraph in the *Times*, which states that Fonthill cost me a million. The love of the world for any thing but the truth, is as great as ever—can you credit such an absurdity? Now I will tell you what it did cost to a shilling."

He rang the bell, and desired his steward might be sent to him. The servant returned, and announced that the steward was not within.

"No matter," said Mr. Beckford, "as the *Times* reckons wholesale, I can tell you to within a thousand pounds—that will do. My whole outlay on Fonthill was 273,000*l.*, some hundreds over that sum it may be, no more. This was scattered over sixteen or eighteen years in the expenditure. The old house at Fonthill was in a low and unhealthy spot, which was the reason of my changing to the new building."

"The fall of the tower was an unfortunate accident," I observed.

"I apprehended it. I feared that some day I should be crushed like a lobster in my shell. They had neglected to secure the foundation; the foreman hinted that the tower was very insecure. Good heaven!" said I, "what is to be done? Cannot any means be adopted to render it safe—we might buttress up the foundation in some way? The answer was 'No, nothing but taking down and rebuilding it from the foundation will do.' This was unwelcome news. The tower was more than two hundred and sixty feet high. I was housed in the new building. It was a source of continual apprehension to me. I was like Damocles with the sword over his head. Perhaps the immediate cause of the fall was something that had gone on within, that imparted a shock a few hours, or it may be a day before it took place. The architects were not only negligent, but obstinate. They would balustrade the bottom of the open window, or rather cloister, at the top of the octagon room on one

* The sum of 5000 guineas was paid for it to Mr. Beckford by government.

side of the passage—a thing very unsuited to a gothic edifice. That room was a hundred and twenty feet high. This annoyed me a good deal. One day I went up with a new pair of these kind of boots on, and planting my back firmly against the inner side of the passage, I kicked with all my might against the top of the ballustrade again and again. Soon loosening the stones, down they went a hundred feet, crash upon the floor beneath, covering the furniture with broken rubbish. The balustrade was then replaced with shields and more suitable designs. I gave them a lesson."

"It must have caused you much pain to quit such a building, and find it so soon dilapidated," I observed.

"Not so much as you might think. I can bend to fortune. I have philosophy enough not to cry like a child about a plaything. The chancellor took away from me by a decree, in the course of what lawyers call justice, two large estates that had been sixty and more years in my family. You may imagine their importance when I tell you that there were fifteen hundred* slaves upon them. This decree, too, the chancellor accompanied with the reflection that 'Mr. Beckford had plenty of property left.' That was my reason for quitting Fonthill. I was sorry to throw many poor people out of employ, and to stay further improvements, but I had no choice—living there would have been too expensive."

Finding Mr. Beckford so affable and communicative, I asked whether it was true that he had built the wall round Fonthill in a year. It was seven or eight miles in extent, I believe, and twelve feet high. He replied that the contract ran for a year, but on the contractor representing that he should be ruined if bound to the original day of completion, he had a month or six weeks more conceded to him, in which time the wall was completed.

"Some persons say," he continued, "that I built the wall before I began the house, to cut myself wholly off from mankind. Why, I had always one, sometimes two hundred workmen with me. I built the wall because I would not have my grounds intruded upon by sportsmen. In vain were they warned off. Your country gentlemen will transport a pauper for taking a few twigs from a hedge, which they will break down without ceremony. They will take no denial when they go hooting in their red jackets, to excruciate to death a poor hare. I found remonstrances vain, so I built the wall to exclude them. I never suffer an animal to be killed but through necessity. Early in life I gave up shooting because I consider we have no right to murder animals for sport. I am fond of animals. The birds in the plantations of Fonthill seemed to know me—they continued their songs as I rode close to them—the very hares grew bold. It was exactly what I wished."

"A story has been circulated that some one came in over the wall, and mistaking the master for the gardener, was shown the grounds, and was at night desired to find his way out as he got in."

"I will tell you the origin of that story. Vulgar curiosity was so excited by the edifice I was constructing, but more by the falsehoods told of myself, that even 'gentlemen' disguised themselves in workmen's dresses, and got in to see what was doing. It was not pleasant, being

* I incline to think I am correct here, though the number seems great.

among the workmen continually, to be looked in the face all day long by intrusive people who had no business there. I never refused strangers at proper seasons, the satisfaction of their curiosity. The circumstance to which you allude has foundation in fact. I was coming out of the hall, going towards the plantations, when a stranger addressed me.

"'Can I see Fonthill?'

"'It is not shown.'

"'Might I see the gardens then? You can show them, I dare say?'

"I thought I would follow out the joke, as the stranger was of gentlemanly address. I led him into the gardens, showed him the grounds, and lastly took him to the house. Here, I imagined, he began to suspect I was not what I pretended. I know not to this day who he was—but I thought him one of the pleasantest men I had ever conversed with—deeply read, sensible, and perfectly well bred. When I had shown him the principal apartments, I knew that dinner was serving up. I begged him to walk with me into a room he had not seen, and instantly led the way to the dinner-table, telling him of his mistake, of which there was by this time little need. I would take no denial; he dined with me. We conversed on a variety of subjects—he was at home in all. When he rose to go away, I rung for a servant, as it was dark, thanking him for his society. I asked if he had any conveyance. He only expressed a wish to be shown the way to the park gate. We parted, and I never saw him more. As to my treating one of the most agreeable strangers I ever saw in my life with rudeness—one who had eaten my salt—it was impossible. I hope I am a gentleman."

I remarked that such misrepresentations arose from ignorance of his mode of living.

"Why distort facts? we must oppose received opinion in nothing if we would be unobserved and free of misrepresentation—our associations must be every body's—we must tacitly assent to falsehoods and frauds. People live now by each other's example altogether. A sort of universalism governs—we act, think, dream in the mass. Soon no single voice will be listened to—there will be no solitary searcher after truth in any thing. What the many do or dream will be the law. Past truths have been the result of individual efforts alone—no great truths have ever been discovered by masses of people—it is fair to suppose they never will. Great truths are the result of knowledge and reflection in minds highly gifted."

"Or universal experience goes for nothing if your remark be not correct," I observed.

"Speaking of the people," said Mr. Beckford, "I should have been happy to serve them had it been in my power. I belong, as my father did, to the popular side."

"Your name could never have been agreeable to the court; yet I saw in an old court magazine for 1782, an account of your going down the country-dance at St. James's with Miss North, on the Queen's birthday," I rejoined.

"I remember it. I was in my twenty-second year—the year before my marriage. In 1780, two years before that, a week after Lord George Gordon's riots in the city, I went to court with some of my opposition friends, who said if we did not go, the king would declare we were all leagued with Lord George. We went to keep up appearances on that occasion. I was too young to be an object of antipathy, or to take any part in politics, during my father's life. Was not his reply to the king bold?"

I replied that I had several times read it with admiration. "Did he, (Mr. Beckford), not think that the public were much deceived in the character of George III.? Lord Chatham had characterised him as capable of the grossest duplicity."

"He was destitute of feeling, too," said Mr. Beckford. "I went to the levee after Gordon's riot, as I have observed. The military had just fired upon the mob—a necessary step to put a stop to lawless plunder and violence. I entered as the king had come out of his closet, the officer who commanded the troops being immediately before me. As soon as the king saw him, he said, 'You peppered them well, I hope—peppered them well—peppered them well!' in his loud way. Every body looked—the levity of the remark struck the officer. Firing even upon lawless mobs was then considered to be justified only by self-evident necessity. 'I hope your majesty's troops will always do their duty,' was the answer, drily returned, with a gravity which feelings less obtuse than the king's must have felt to be a tacit reproof, as many were killed."

"Lord North's correspondence, recently published, shifts the prolongation of the American war upon the king," I added

"It clears North of all but weakness in suffering the king to sacrifice him to the royal obstinacy. Yet the royal declaration, not long before its sincerity, so unhappily for the king, was brought to the test, that he would lay down his crown before he would acknowledge American independence, might have deceived ministers more gifted with penetration than Lord North. I have no doubt Pitt was driven into the war with France. The abandonment of his early principles that as a minister made him so popular, the violent measures he pursued, and his swamping the House of Lords with new creations, was the king's determination, he being the instrument."

"He might have resigned."

"Pitt loved power—he was proud—but he had not the pride of his father, who, a courtier in manners and fond of power too, would not have suffered the king to rob him of his self-respect. His ambition was more honourable."

"I have often thought there was more meaning in Pitt's dying exclamation than every body understood," I observed.

"It is not improbable—Pitt was my companion in our minority. He was a year older than I am. I used to visit for days together at Burton Pynsent."

"Lord Chatham, I believe, took great pains with Pitt's education?"

"I remember," said Mr. Beckford, "he was very particular about the words he used in conversation. I arrived once at Lord Chatham's, when William Pitt had been absent on a visit, but was hourly expected home. I was in the apartment with the father when his son came in. 'I hope you have spent your time agreeably, William?' said the earl. 'Most delectably,' replied William Pitt. Lord Chatham put on one of his stern looks—sternly, indeed, with his eagle features he could look when he pleased. 'Delectably, sir? Never let me hear you utter that affected word again. Delectably, sir!'"

(*To be continued.*)

RECOLLECTIONS OF THE AUTHOR OF "VATHEK."

BY CYRUS REDDING, ESQ.

(*Concluded from page* 158.)

THE conversation respecting the Pitt family continued. Burton Pynsent, the gift of Sir William Pynsent to Lord Chatham, was sold by his elder son John Pitt, the last earl, known by the *soubriquet* of "the *late* Earl of Chatham," from his spending the best part of the day in bed. The earl, who is now only remembered as the chosen of Lord Castlereagh to command the Walcheren expedition, where both the statesman and soldier earned pretty nearly the same measure of renown, parted with the estate, bequeathed to his father by private gratitude, to pay debts contracted at play. The column erected by Lord Chatham to Sir William Pynsent's memory, was doomed to be pulled down and sold for the value of the materials. Some gentlemen of the vicinity, indignant at the proceeding, clubbed the value of this monument among themselves, and preserved it for posterity, out of respect to the memory of the great statesman. Mr. Beckford was perhaps the only living individual who had a recollection of Lords Chatham and Lyttleton, as personal acquaintance. Lord Camden, another of his father's friends, survived until 1794, and is remembered by many. He spoke with feeling of the kindness these noble lords extended to him in his youth after his father was no more. Lord Camden he called the "Cato of the bench;" nothing could shake his integrity. He voted for Lord Chatham's celebrated motion in the House of Peers. The king took away the seals from his conscience keeper for this. The bar behaved most honourably upon the occasion. For some time no one would take the seals. Mr. Yorke, who first accepted the office, was seized with such remorse in consequence, that he put an end to his own life before a peerage patent could be got ready for him.

"A little accident," said Mr. Beckford, "that would hardly happen in the present day among the aspirants for the office of royal conscience keeper—*circumspice!*"

Multifarious as were the books and MSS. he possessed, he found in an instant whatever he sought, the organ of "order" being well developed in his cranium, to borrow the phrase of phrenological empiricism. He rang for no servant if what he wanted happened to be in another apartment, but fetched it himself, every volume in his vast collection, every picture and drawing, having their locality familiar. He brought forward a portfolio containing letters to himself, of William Pitt in his boyhood, and one or two written by Lord Chatham. The great statesman, unless when "thumb-screwed" with gout, haughty as he was in public, exhibited great kindness and affability in private. "We exercised ourselves in writing, carrying on a fictitious correspondence. I might have preserved many notes of that time highly interesting; one does not understand in youth what trifles time may change into gold."

Though but seventeen when Lord Chatham died, he well remembered the state of the public mind in regard to him. He observed, that it was impossible to judge of the respect in which that great man was held, by any display of public feeling towards a political character of recent days. The king hated and feared him; his conduct, about America, regained him the popularity he lost by accepting a peerage.

"Lord Chatham outlived my father, and lost a devoted admirer. What chief magistrate of London, before or since my father, ever gave a single entertainment at the Mansion House which cost ten thousand pounds of his own money? My father's speech was not written by Wilkes as some have asserted. His recollection was good. He was at Westminster school with Lords Mansfield and Kinnoul. These three were dubbed "the Triumvirate," being the best verse-makers in the school. He was a bad speaker, but able to write, and was a very intrepid man. Feeling indignant at the insult the king had put upon the city by laughing when an address was presented, he determined it should not pass unregarded. The king was as much surprised as angry at the rejoinder. Lord Chatham was too high-minded for George III., who was a man of coarse feelings. High-minded noblemen are not royal favourites. The subject must not touch the hem of the royal robe. I have seen something of courts; both here and abroad. There must be no competition with regality—all must be prostrate to fatten upon its good things. Did you ever see William Pitt?"

"The boards of his coffin," I replied. "I was one of three hundred admitted by the dean's tickets into the Abbey at his funeral. I remember seeing Lord Chatham's coffin, which, on opening the vault, they said was found upon its side; some observed, it was to turn his back upon his son. I had never seen the Abbey until that day."

"I should scarcely dare to look into that grave; all the past would rush upon me; melancholy recollections would haunt me afterwards. William Pitt had great abilities; but he wanted the grand soul of his father. I have lost many friends whose remembrance comes too forcibly upon me. Look into my letters. I lost them, and became afraid to acquire more, lest I should lose them in turn. When I last went to Portugal, what changes a short time had made! It was subsequently to that time when I visited Mr. Beauchamp, whom you recollect."

I replied I was too young; I had spoken only of Pengreep, his seat—I did not recollect the master.

"Well, when I passed a day or two at Pengreep, the weather in March was soft and fine, as in Portugal. I sat there making a looking-glass of the water, full of vehement hopes, anticipating the orange-groves of Portugal, and amusement, which at that time I much wanted. I was a young widower. I found all these, and what are they become—friendships—all you read of my friends, dark cloudy thoughts that accidental circumstances call up with intolerable bitterness."

Here for a few moments he was silent, talking to himself, as was his habit, when alone. Indeed, for a minute or two I do not think he was conscious of my being present. This habit of talking to himself he had when riding or walking out of doors.

"I mentioned that Dr. Wolcot told me his friend, Governor Trelawney, could not look in Pitt's (Lord Chatham's) face in the House of Commons; that his eyes nailed him to the floor."

"Truly characteristic—his nose, too, was like an eagle's beak, ready to tear open his prey—you knew Wolcot?"

"For many of his last years I spent some time with him every week."

"He was old when he died?"

"About eighty-five."

"The *Quarterly Review* had a very abusive article upon him after his decease, I recollect."

"Gifford knew its allegations were false—they had been enemies—the article affected to deplore Wolcot's end in poverty and wretchedness, a sort of judgment upon him for satirising people of condition. Shield, the composer, several artists, Lord Coventry, blind too, used to visit him, to the last. Gifford knew Wolcot had an annuity from the booksellers; he had some small property besides which came on the decease of a sister; he never spent his income, and at his death left duty-paid legacies to his two servants."

"Tell me more about him."

Here I went at length into a history of all I knew of Wolcot. Mr. Beckford listened with great attention, seeming in a reverie.

"You call up mournful remembrances. Wolcot was the most delightful company I ever knew. He charmed my visiters at Fonthill with his wit and story-telling—he knew the two worlds well—men and books—he knew both, as I do—he came to see me with Lord Nelson."

"That was many years ago.?"

"Nearly forty—yes, forty—*labitur et labetur!* Sir William Hamilton, whom you see is in my sketches, I first knew in Naples. I was not more than twenty years of age then. Sir William came home to retire from his duties after thirty-six years of service. He rode the antiquarian hobby, as you know, but he understood his *ménege.* What a house his was at Naples! There were all the clever people, the artists, the antiquaries, musicians, the beauty and gaiety of the city. It was my home. Lady Hamilton was a charming creature—I do not mean 'the Nelson.' The dawn of life then was as bright as the bay on which I looked every morning, and making allowance for its vivid feelings, I say truth when I speak of Lady Hamilton as an angel of purity. She lived, uncorrupted, in the midst of the Neapolitan court. You must have known what the court was, to comprehend this in its full meaning. I never saw so heavenly-minded a creature. Her power of musical execution was miraculous—so sweetly soft was her touch—she seemed as if she had thrown her own essence into the music. I used to listen to her like one entranced. She died in 1782—but I go from the point. Sir William Hamilton was near seventy when he came home. I invited him to Fonthill. He had married the too-famous Lady Hamilton, who survived him. She was, nobody knew who—she came with Sir William. Lord Nelson and Wolcot arrived together—many people were visiting me at the same time. I gave a sort of fête at the abbey, only then half finished. Lady Hamilton figured there before Lord Nelson, much to her own satisfaction, in the character of Agrippina—it should have been Cleopatra. She represented the character well—I must do her that justice. Perhaps Nelson inspired her. Wolcot enjoyed the scene greatly, and entertained every body with his conversation. A pressing engagement called him away after a week's visit, and I never saw him again. How well he wrote—how original his style and humour. He understood character thoroughly—he played with human foibles! He repeated an epigram on his setting a nightcap on fire, he had borrowed of Lord Nelson, while sitting up reading.* Sir William Hamilton, my old friend, died two or three years after this visit. Some of his finest antiquities are in the Museum."

"Was the second Lady Hamilton a fascinating woman?"

"I never thought her so; she was somewhat masculine, but symmetrical in figure, so that Sir William called her his Grecian. Her countenance was agreeable—certainly not beautiful. She affected sensibility, but felt none—was artful; and no wonder, she had been trained in the court of Naples—a fine school for an Englishwoman of any stamp. It was a hell of corruption. Nelson was infatuated. She could make him believe any thing—that the profligate queen was a Madonna. He was her dupe. She persuaded him at last that she had a daughter—a Nelsoness. She never had a child in her life, in the opinion of those who knew something about her. She rivetted Nelson's heart by telling him it was through her means his ships were fitted and victualled. The fact was, no minister had ever such a preponderating influence at the court of Naples as Sir William Hamilton—it was his affair. He had been all-powerful there long before he saw his second wife."

"There was the breach of treaty, and the murder of Carraciola afterwards."

"We must veil that horrible affair," said Mr. Beckford. "It will not bear repetition—it is a melancholy incident in history."

Speaking of Mr. Hope and Anastasius, he declared it was a considerable time before he could believe that story was written by him. Hope exhibited less apparent capacity for the production of so fine a thing than any author he had known. He had read the work again and again. The fidelity of colouring—the perfect delineation of Greek character—the knowledge of detail—the mind displayed, made it a matter of mystery to him in some degree still. That any one should live to be old before he produced a literary work of such a high character, was surprising; the world was full of miracles. Mr. Hope's "upholstery book" was no promising precursor of such a tale—it would for ever puzzle him how it happened. "What a fine passage," said he, "was that descriptive of the ruin of Euphrosyne—how heart rending!" I was obliged to lay down the book when I read it the first time before I got to the conclusion—it was agonising—the picture is worked up to indescribable hor-

---

* In Peter Pindar's works :—

> "Take your nightcap again, my good lord, I desire,
> For I will not keep it a minute;
> What belongs to a Nelson, where'er there's a fire,
> Is sure to be instantly in it."

Wolcot had lashed Sir William, for his antiquarian enthusiasm, in some of his odes several years before.

† Mr. Beckford was sensitive—acted strongly upon by external things full of emotion. He was humane and charitable, giving away considerable sums, but would not permit his name to appear as a donor. In one instance, where he presented two

ror. I asked myself if human nature could reach such a pitch of depravity as is painted there; yet it no doubt has done so. We find horrors in real life beyond the dreams of fiction.† Hope's work is singular—strange. What admirable keeping—the real test of authorship in novel writing. Just keeping is a secret towards success few attain. Educated persons see glaring discrepancies that escape the generality of readers in this respect, and fling away the work half read—it exhausts patience. The ladies who so admirably hit off the follies of society, and describe social life so well, fail in attempting, indeed, what they have no business to try. They cannot describe naval life or military operations—Greece and Rome puzzle them—they are always caught tripping at consuls and senators."

" Men make the ancients their study in youth," I remarked.

"Yet even of men how few succeed. Lockhart has done well in 'Valerius'—Bulwer has failed altogether in his 'Pompeii'—there is nothing Roman in the writer or his characters."

Meeting him afterwards at a flower show in Sidney Gardens I mentioned that I was going into Monmouthshire, and should in my way visit the observatory at Clifton, where I had heard there were some fine telescopes. Mr. Beckford would be glad, to hear how I liked the scenery, and what state the observatory was in. On my return, he inquired which of the ruins I preferred.

I replied " Tintern."

" O, but the castles ?"

"Chepstow."

" Not Ragland ?"

I answered in the negative, because Ragland was made a show place. " Wyatt had been set to 'improve' the ruin."

"Improve a ruin!—Wyatt? Time is ruin's architect—so Ragland has been Wyatted. I saw it then before it was 'improved.' What have they done!"

"Removed the fallen fragments—kept the greensward where they fell neat and trim for walking upon—set up a stone table, with timber legs fluted, in the roofless hall—you feel in a moment art has been intermeddling. Chepstow has been left to time and storm. Then there is the dungeon of Martin to interest by association."

"Martin's prison was something like Bonnivard's, close to the water. Martin was long enough there to exclaim, as well as he—

---

hundred pounds, it was on the sole condition that it should be placed on the subscription list as from A. B. A young man shewed considerable abilities as a scholar, a total stranger, but now a distinguised professor. Upon hearing that his father could not afford to send him to the university, Mr. Beckford presented the necessary means unsolicited. It was seldom he would permit his name to appear in the list of subscriptions to a literary work. Even in his almsgiving there was a peculiarity. One day as he was riding near Bath, he was struck by seeing a miserable object in the road who had lost both legs. The man did not beg, perhaps from fear of one of those laws so little creditable to legislative humanity, that as the quantum of misery increases, deems it good policy to sharpen its intensity. He pulled up his horse, not knowing that he was observed but by his groom. "Poor fellow, you must be miserable indeed !" Then putting his hand into his pocket, and flinging down to the dismembered man whatever money met his grasp, without looking at it—sovereigns and silver together—he rode onwards.

It was the same at length to me,
Fettered or fetterless to be.

I knew Bonnivard's prison, and have spent hours near, watching the tumbling waters that were precipitated into the lake, or soothing my ears with the ripple of the waves against the shore, dreaming of all that was lovely to me of which I had been deprived.* Ragland came by marriage to the Somersets in 1520. It is long since I saw it. Your 'improved' ruin puts me in mind of one shattered by lightning in the grounds of Mount Edgcumbe, which its lord ordered to be repaired! What of the observatory?"

"It is not completed. I looked through a fine refracting telescope, but there was too much dancing vapour in the air to see distant objects well. There is no reflector yet set up—the size of a reflector, half as large again as Herchel's forty-feet instrument, was spoken of—might not a house be seen with it in the moon?"

Mr. Beckford was delighted.

"I repent never having studied astronomy. There is a touch of astrology in 'Vathek,' I believe; but astrology is a very obscure science, adept in it as I am pronounced to be by many. Except what every body knows of the stars, I know nothing. I wish I was better acquainted with some of those distant worlds. Ten years younger, and I would build an observatory on the point of Lansdown towards the Avon, three hundred feet high, furnish it with instruments, and shut myself up until I was master of the science. I am too old now—I must think less of this planet—

Le cerf volante dont le ficelle casse,
Tourne en tombant tourne et tombe toujours!

Ours is a miserable atom of creation—we and all our solar system—amidst the many that dot and sparkle along the infinity of space. How much is to be discovered! How few of these magnificent worlds will glasses ever enable man to see? What sort of people inhabit them? Is life there—death—original corruption, which Dr. Whitby wrote so well against? I lament my ignorance of astronomy—I cannot learn it now—we do not live half long enough to acquire the hornbook of the studies life opens to us."

This allusion to shutting up in the observatory recalled to my memory that I heard Mr. Beckford purchased Gibbon's library at Lausanne, and shut himself in it for a long time.

"I bought it to have something to read when I passed through Lausanne. I have not been there since. I shut myself up for six weeks, from early in the morning until night, only now and then taking a ride. The people thought me mad. I read myself nearly blind."

I inquired if the books were rare or curious. He replied in the negative. There were excellent editions of the principal historical writers, and an extensive collection of travels. The most valuable work was an edition of "Eustathius;" there was also a MS. or two. All the books were in excellent condition; in number, considerably above six thousand, near

* His wife, Lady Margaret died at the Château de la Tour, not far away, just after lying in. He is said to have vowed he would be faithful to her memory and never marry again.

seven perhaps. He should have read himself mad if there had been novelty enough, and he had stayed much longer.

"I broke away and dashed among the mountains. There is excellent reading there, too, equally to my taste. Did you ever travel alone among mountains?"

I replied that I had, and been fully sensible of their mighty impressions. "Do you retain Gibbon's library?"

"It is now dispersed, I believe. I made it a present to my excellent physician, Dr. Schall or Scholl." (I am not certain of the name.) "I never saw it after turning hermit there."

I remarked that I had seen some of his notes in books sold at Fonthill.

"I sold but little of what I valued, there," he replied. "I had not room enough for all the books I possessed in any other place. Do not suppose more than half of what was sold at Fonthill was mine. I disposed of my superfluous furniture, for which I had no use, and also of some costly things, not of much utility—suitable there only. I would not disgrace my house by Chinese furniture—that was not mine—it was put in by the auctioneer. Horace Walpole would not have suffered it in his toyshop of Strawberry Hill. Did you ever see Strawberry Hill?"

"Only the outside. I was nearly drowned there among the weeds, swimming across the Thames."

"Walpole hated me. I began Fonthill two or three years before his death. Mischief-making people annoyed him by saying I intended to buy up all his nic-nackery when he was dead. Some things I might have wished to possess—a good deal I would not have taken as a gift. The place was a miserable child's box—a species of gothic mousetrap—a reflection of Walpole's littlenesses. I happened to be adding to the Fonthill collection of pictures at the time, and was made a bugbear of. Mrs. Damer and Lord Waldegrave may thank me for their legacy. My having his playthings he could not tolerate, even in idea, so he bequeathed them beyond my reach, as he not improbably surmised. I was thirty-seven when he died—mortals grope in the dark. He built every thing upon family honours and gossip—his writings are portraits of himself. He would have abused my heraldic emblazonments at Fonthill. He was full of spleen. He would have written and talked me and my buildings down to the ground—yet he affected the philosopher."

"The painted glass at Fonthill was preserved?"

"It was made for the building, and went with it—it was appropriate there—nowhere else. Mine is a family of some standing—I had the quarterings properly executed. The heralds traced me up to a Norman cobbler;* there they stopped. Heraldry is a useful study before the time when the visitations ceased in 1620. Since that date the heralds have dispersed a vast quantity of spurious gentility. Did you know old Sir Isaac Heard?"

I replied in the negative.

"Heard once came to me full of tribulation, to consult about an application for arms made to him by the distant relation of a peer

* A joke upon Oliver de Crespin, steward of Normandy, to whom, by the mother's side, his ancestry was traced.

who had succeeded to the honours. He wished to have his own arms quartered with those of the peerage. Heard hunted until he was tired to death—no arms could he trace to that branch of the family. 'What shall I do?' said Sir Isaac, 'what shall I do, Mr. Beckford?' I was hard at work at the time studying heraldry. 'Do,' I replied, 'why, as he never had arms, help him out—make him some.'"

"'Mr. Beckford!' said Heard, with affected surprise.

"'No coyness, Heard, make them. What do you do for good citizens who get into corporate offices?'

"'We search.'

"'But you don't find?'

"'We are often not consulted at all—the coachmaker puts on something.'

"'You asked my advice—make them—don't lose a warm fee for the lack of finding materials—I will invent them for you.'

"Sir Isaac could not help laughing—a quartering appeared from somewhere—what revelation had been made to Heard I never discovered. Those who had not arms before 1620 must have grants, in order to be regular. I was at one time fond of the study. You know that by my mother's side I was a Hamilton?—you remember Grammont's 'Hamilton?'—what a charming book is that! He was an ancestor of mine by the Abercorn family."

"I went once from Tunbridge to Summer Hill to see a place so much spoken about in Grammont," I observed; "it belonged to a banker."

"The old house has long been pulled down I suppose. Modern herald's do not associate in appearance with the notion of an old herald and his paraphernalia—they should look of 1620 at least."

"I do not comprehend."

"Oh they are smart fellows now, fresh as their newly emblazoned vert, gules, or azure. They do not seem in character with old times—we should snuff the charnel house about them—they should look yellow, worm-eaten keepers of musty parchments—a herald should resemble a rusty dry bones."

His general temperament seemed cheerful, but was evidently, even in his age, that of one who ran to an excess in every thing—and was accustomed to have all he desired. Extremely kind in friendship, he was implacable in his resentments; passionate; reserved by nature; proud and impetuous on exciting occasions; to some all gentlemanly frankness and affability, to others distance and etiquette. In youth he was said to have been remarkable for bashfulness. Hence many opposite descriptions of his bearing are given. He shaped his conduct after the position of the party whom he addressed, having a thorough knowledge of the world. He was willing, though many say not, to oblige strangers with a sight of his buildings and grounds, but was so overcome with applications and letters from all kinds of persons, as well as with impertinencies, that he ordered his steward to open and return all letters from strangers that he the steward did not think of moment, giving him any the handwriting of which was identified. A trayful of letters was sometimes taken in from the door of a morning. He never refused permission to see his property when the application came to him through one of whom he had the slightest knowledge. He would not tax his time merely to gratify idle curiosity, and herein was scarcely to be blamed when the extent of that curiosity was so considerable and often so purposeless. To return to his conversation.

He had been speaking of Selden. I had recently seen the house in which Selden was born, and showed him a small sketch, shaded rather blackly with pencil.

"It is humble, indeed," he observed; "you have made the light and shade Rembrandtish. I like such effects however rough. What a glorious fellow the Dutchman was, without grace or beauty. He threw about his light like another sun. What an expressive colourist—what strength he had—the very Samson of art—his native dykes and dams stagnating all. How unfortunate that the nature he copied partook of his mental constitution—he revelled in Dutch grossness, but even that he made the most astonishing thing in painting—he was a miracle in his day, he is so still—he will be so for ever; but let me show you a sketch I have made for an observatory."

He produced some outlines in which every convenience was provided for astronomical instruments. There seemed to be abundant room for every thing required, except the large reflector of which we had spoken. Nothing could be more simply applicable. Architectural design was evidently familiar to him. I observed that a dome was wanting over all, for the reflector.

"No," he observed, "an instrument of sixty feet focus would not answer there; we must consider the elevation, three hundred feet. We must have the reflector upon the brow of the hill close by—there it is all a *château en Espagne!*"

Among other incidents he related was one respecting the late Duchess of Gordon, so well known for her shrewd boldness; and sticking at nothing to serve her purposes, which were generally too notoriously palpable to be mistaken. He had spoken of shutting himself up at Lausanne.

"I once shut myself up at Fonthill to be out of the way of a lady,—an ungallant thing, I allow, to any lady on earth but her with whom it occurred. You must well remember the late Duchess of Gordon, as she was the continual talk of the town for her curious ways. I could have served no other lady so I hope—I never enjoyed a joke so much. At that time every body talked of Mr. Beckford's enormous wealth—every thing about me was exaggerated proportionately. I was in consequence a capital bait for the duchess's bite—so she thought;—I thought differently. She had been told that even a dog kennel at Fonthill was a palace—my house a Potosi. What more upon earth could be desired by a managing mother for a daughter. I might have been aged and impotent—no matter, such is fashion's philosophy. I got a hint of her intention to surprise me with her hard face at Fonthill—a sight I could gladly dispense with. I determined not to see her. I resolved to give her a lesson. Fonthill was put in order for her reception, with every thing I could devise to receive her magnificently—not only to receive her, but to turn the tables upon her for the presumption she had that I was to become the plaything of her purposes."

"The splendour of her reception must have stimulated her in her object."

"I designed it should operate in that manner. I knew her aim pretty well—she little thought so. My arrangements being made I ordered my '*mayordomo*' to say, on the duchess's arrival, that it was unfortunate— every thing being arranged for her grace's reception, Mr. Beckford had shut himself up on a sudden, a way he had at times, and that it was more than his place was worth to disturb him, as his master only appeared when he pleased, forbidding interruption, even if the king came to Fonthill. I had just received a new stock of books, and had them removed to the rooms of which I had taken possession. The duchess conducted herself with wonderful equanimity, and seemed much surprised and gratified at what she saw, and the mode of her reception—just as I desired she should be. When she got up in the morning, her first question was, 'Do you think Mr. Beckford will be visible to-day ?'

" 'I cannot inform your grace—Mr. Beckford's movements are so very uncertain—it is possible. Would your grace take an airing in the park —a walk in the gardens ?'

"Every thing which Fonthill could supply was made the most of, whetting her appetite to her purpose still more. My master of the ceremonies to the duchess did not know what to make of his master, the duchess, or his own position. 'Perhaps Mr. Beckford will be visible to-morrow ?' was the duchess's daily consolation. To-morrow, and to-morrow, and to-morrow, came and went—no Mr. Beckford ! I read on, determined not to see her. Was it not serving right such a woman as she was ? She could not play the speculator with me."

She remained, I think Mr. Beckford said, seven or eight days, magnificently entertained, and then went away without seeing him. She was very angry, and said all sorts of scandalous things about him afterwards. —"Think of such a woman's vengeance ; such a woman as the duchess was, who never suffered any thing to stand in the way of her objects !"

The splendour and wealth she saw dispensed at Fonthill no doubt increased her disappointment, and enhanced the bitterness of the contumely she afterwards heaped upon him.

Mr. Beckford was one day reading a translation of some Hindu dramas ; I think they were those translated by Wilson a few years ago. He inquired if I had seen them ? In reply I lamented being unacquainted with eastern literature, except through one or two translations by Jones and others. I added that I had a catalogue of Sanscrit and other eastern MSS. in my possession, given me by the late Sir William Ousely. Mr. Beckford not having seen it, I sent it to Lansdown to be at his service. The next day he sent me all his printed works, including the third edition of his sketches, which contains, so he wrote in the book itself, a page or two more than those which preceded it. He thanked me for the catalogue, but "ten times more" for a little volume, then out of print, descriptive of the Alps, "recalling them vividly to his recollection," and inviting me to Lansdown that we might talk over the scenery.

I found him in his library taking down a book. "Here I am, as usual, nestled among all the good things that intellect has produced—my walls are 'instinct' with thought—I inhale here the essence of departed wisdom—the breathings of its spirit." He was looking for the trial of Sydney.

"Did you never remark," said he, "that there was no such thing as a fair trial in political cases until of late years. Juries were only the tools of the judges—the judges tools of the court—the innocence or guilt of the party was an indifferent affair. The original object of trial by jury was subverted by the judges. For ages a trial for treason was a mere farce—the *finale* being whatever the court desired it should be—the judge a sort of agent for the court, the jury the servants of the judge. The jury under the good old Saxon institutions were themselves the judges. It is surprising how stupid the people were to their rights, from not being able to regulate such things by concert and their own power. Of all judicial proceedings I ever hit upon, that of the court of Thoulouse was the most edifying. They executed the prisoner under a sentence admitting his innocence—there was something more honest about it than in our old mode of management in state trials."

"I do not know it," I interrupted.

"'Mr. Teronde,' said the judge, 'the court does not find you guilty in the least; but being well informed of your inmost thoughts, have condemned you to be beheaded and your estate confiscated.' You will find the case in the ecclesiastical history of the reformed churches of France —it happened in the 'sixteenth century.'"

A MS. lay on the table. "That," said Mr. Beckford, "is my 'Liber Veritatis.' I pull the peerage about sadly. I have recently amused myself by examining the claims of the peerage to be 'gentlemen;' in the heraldic sense I mean. You cannot think how few there are who can claim ancestral honours, yet all pretend to do so the moment they get a coronet. Nobles in the heraldic sense are not peers exclusively; they are those only who bear a coat of arms, the older the more noble—they need not have a title at all. A minister may make a peer of any body, but he can only through the crown make him a noble of inferior rank to a country gentleman whose family has long borne arms. On the continent a count may take precedence of a prince, not of a royal line, if he be a noble of older standing. There are not more than thirty of the old nobility in the house—why pretend it is otherwise. A peer of to-day, it is true, will do for legislative objects."

Mr. Beckford then proceeded to quote examples of the mode in which peers had been made—the "why" and "wherefore"—exceedingly amusing. He knew the history of every peer carved out of late years, and gave some curious examples of their recommendation to ministerial *beneficence* with their qualifications; clever and caustic. Two thirds of the House of Peers had been added in his time. The old peerage of the country was sunk beneath ministerial creations for political ends.

"Where was the system to stop? The constitution had been abused. Any minister might destroy the independence of the House of Lords, as had been done under George III., to cripple opposition to his extravagant and ruinous wars. I have nearly finished my work—every syllable is true. I must not publish it. Truth is a bitter draught."

"But the publication may do good."

"It might—the peerage is become dog-cheap. At the present rate of creations the House will soon require Westminster Hall for a place of meeting. A peerage in this great country should be a distinction envied by men of likelihood and pretension in the first instance."

On taking leave of this singularly gifted man, he said, "Where are

---

* The "Liber Veritatis" was afterwards changed in title I believe to the "Book of Folly." It bore well on the above points, which were conversational—the severity of the censure of some inconsistencies (rather personal) will most likely prevent its publication.

you going?" I replied to town. "I have a house in Park-lane, the entrance in Park-street. I shall be most happy to see you there." I called upon him accordingly. One day I picked up a copy of "Huerte" from a shop window, where it lay open at a page that contained two lines upon a subject on which we had recently been conversing. Mr. Beckford had never seen the edition—I wished he would accept and add it to his collection of Spanish books, and came to tell him so. He was not within. I left a note, which, besides speaking of "Huerte," expressed my surprise at seeing a paragraph in the *Morning Chronicle* which had so close a relation to a subject on which we had been conversing, I feared he might imagine it had come from me. I stated my utter ignorance of any person connected in the remotest way with the publication. He replied by note—

"There is nothing to pick off that dry bone 'Huerte,' but the passage you have noted, which is really curious. The little paragraph squeezed into the *Morning Chronicle*, I am told, was copied, *literatim et verbatim* from the *Herald*. Who sent it thither I cannot conjecture; but I am most certain, from internal evidence, it was not you.

"If you happen to be disengaged next Sunday morn., about twelve, pray come to me, and I will read the Vathek episodes to you in part. These I may possibly soon publish, but I cannot bring myself to let out the 'Liber Veritatis'—*ce n'est pas toute verité qui est bonne à dire!*"

Such an invitation was not to be missed. I was in Park-street just after church time. Mr. Beckford spoke again of Byron's great anxiety to see these episodes, which is found in the poet's correspondence. He expected the Duke of Hamilton, and would wait a little before commencing. The duke had heard the episodes once.

"If he comes in you will know his opinion on some of the passages. I speak without partiality, when I say that there are few of a more correct taste, or more capable of giving an opinion upon literary subjects, than the duke. He is reserved by nature; but you will hear what a discriminating perception he possesses. I have marked passages for alteration at his suggestion, and I have great confidence in the soundness of his judgment. He has written nothing. Men of rank, who live at ease, will seldom encounter the toil of writing. There may be talent and inclination without ardour to overcome labour."

The episodes were written on letter-paper, in French, apparently many years ago.

The time drawing on, and the duke not arriving, Mr. Beckford commenced reading. It was a gloomy day in February. He sat back from the window at least two-thirds of the depth of the room. The light was indifferent, and yet with no difficulty he read through both. He stopped but rarely, to make remarks upon particular passages. He was then, I believe, seventy-eight years old, yet wore no spectacles, and read a full hour and a half. He pronounced French with the old court accent. Of the episodes I can say no more, than that they struck me forcibly as possessing much of the character of "Vathek." One of them depicts a beautiful half-angel, half-mortal abstraction, in connection with love, telling admirably in the author's eastern manner. I urged the publication of the episodes while the author was so well able to superintend it himself. He replied, "I will not let the manuscript go under a thousand pounds —I will not let my writings go for nothing."

Here I remarked that those whom his old acquaintance, Peter Pindar, described as eating and drinking out of other men's skulls, would balance the small quantity of manuscripts against the price for which they could afford to sell it to the public. I feared the episodes would make so little in print, and consequently bear so small a price, that the sum he demanded would not, on that account, be paid—I would inquire, if he wished me.

"Do," he replied, "then you will perhaps translate them for me. We can examine the translation by the French afterwards."

I said I felt honoured by his proposition, and would make the requisite inquiry; but it terminated as I foresaw it must.

"They shall not have the MS. under a thousand," said Mr. Beckford.

It is to be hoped these episodes will not be lost to the world. A touch or two in them, I remember, recalled the style of Voltaire. I said as much. He replied, "It was very possible I was right—he thought it might be so."

He told me he had been at his banker's to see if he could afford to purchase the sketches and drawings of Sir Thomas Lawrence's collection.

"I shall keep them in the country," he observed, "if I do no more—they will else be dispersed—I assure you there is nothing like them here, or any where else, to be obtained for money. It is shameful the country does not buy them. Except among a few gentlemen, there is no sound taste for the arts in England. Collections are made from ostentation by people of wealth, who do not know a good from a bad picture. The government is not sensible of the value of art to the nation. It will lavish money upon any thing else, but it grudges money for the arts. A minister picks a committee of taste out of the House of Commons, as he would a committee for any other purpose, and his committee does nothing but blunder. There must be a feeling for art—mere admiration won't do—people admire, andaffect to be struck with works of art, because others affect the same thing. Just as an opera audience cries 'Wonderful!' at a performance of which it does not comprehend a syllable. The beauty of art must be inwardly felt—the mind in it must be read, interpreted. There is Raffaelle—he is at the head of painting every body says—his pictures it is safe to admire and applaud. Ask why Raffaelle is the prince of painters—they cannot tell you. Now an Italian amateur of the lowest order will explain all this, and more. A just taste for art is a cultivated taste; there is no royal road to it, as too many think there is. I am sorry I cannot just now afford to buy the Lawrence collection. I have not 22,000*l.* in my banker's hands to spare. I have been spending money lately."

"In improvements?"

"In planting. I have crowned Lansdown with a forest since you were there."

He seemed delighted with the change he had thus effected.

"With a forest?"

"With a forest—Birnam wood is come to Lansdown. The Bath people may call me a magician, Vathek, or the devil now, with some reason. The Bristol folks who travel the lower road, seeing trees upon Lansdown, where none appeared a few weeks before, rub their eyes—they cannot believe their own sight—how can it be! You have seen my gardener, Vincent—almost as old as myself—equally uncomfortable if idle—he came to me and said,

" 'Now, sir, there is only one thing wanting to make your grounds perfect.'

" 'You want a job, Vincent—what is it?'

" 'Why you have no shade between the two gardens. The sun shines dreadfully hot there in summer—it should be planted, that you might walk in shade all the way up.'

" 'Nonsense, Vincent,' said I; 'before trees can grow up there, where will you and I be?'

" 'Don't say that, sir,' said Vincent; 'you can trust my word—you shall walk up there under the shade of your own trees in the spring——next spring—every tree twelve feet high. If you, sir, find the money, I will find the trees. It is the first week in October, the time to set about it.'

" Well, Vincent,—I will find the money—get to work—get the trees.'

" For many weeks I renewed my old habits. I was out with the work-people from morning till night, planting. There is nothing more for old Vincent to do, unhappily—he will die of *ennui.* You will be surprised at Lansdown forest when you come to Bath. Another year the trees will be all I can desire for shade. I shall have a woodland walk again —I shall hear the spring songs of the birds there, on that hill, where there was only turf so lately. Are you fond of the lark's song—the warble as it mounts in the air?—it is more delightful to me than the song of any other bird."

" There is a peculiar gleesomeness in the lark's song. I have heard it too on the very spot under the 'soft blue sky,' which you describe in one of your letters as mounting from among the herbage, that scented 'the air with the perfume of apricots.' "

" It is the song of a glad innocent heart on a sunny day. I hear it on Lansdown with as much pleasure now as I ever did in my life. Nature never lets us tire—we never forget the love to our mother. Abroad or at home I always gave some time to solitude—in my early youth I disliked large companies—I could not think, it confused my ideas. In Portugal, France, Italy—you know the Alps—you feel them, or your book says wrong—I enjoyed nature most alone. I was enraptured in early life with the country; vanity led me into the circles of fashion. I lived in Switzerland among the Alps; at twenty-six, under a bitter domestic calamity, I found their solitudes soothe me as nothing else would—I have loved solitude more since. I had inexhaustible animal spirits but they never prevented my stealing into temporary peace, beyond the dissipation in which I might be figuring—my letters on Portugal show that—you have read my running away from the gluttons of Batalha and their pampered dinners—what a ride I had that day. Messena and the French burned that superb monastery—it looks well as a ruin I dare say. I should like to see it now—what a lesson it would be to the recollection of former pomps and vanities! Time takes all from us but his hard lessons. My poor dog is dead—my old companion. I expected it before."

I had missed the dog—a spaniel, black and tan colour. I presume it was sent and buried near the tower on Lansdown, where a little marble memorial lay ready to mark the spot, anticipating its interment. The kindness of Mr. Beckford to animals was remarkable. He spoke of Magendie, the celebrated French surgeon, and of surgical experiments, with strong reprehension.

"To what extent the Almighty has carried the sense of feeling and consciousness in animals, our blind eyes cannot see—are we therefore to deny them the exercise of a common humanity? who knows but they have souls as well as we—" was his argument.

I carried him the lines on the picture of St. Catherine, after he had several times asked about them. He took up his pencil and began reading.

"What works I have seen of Raffaelle's!—what religion there is in his paintings!—go any distance out of your way to see pictures of that master—they breathe all they represent—there is an atmosphere of piety around them. His pencil was baptised in the fire of devotion, as that of no other mortal ever was."

"Which do you think his best work?"

"The 'Madonna del Spasimo' at Madrid. I have mentioned it in my 'Sketches'—it produced a more striking effect upon me than any other picture I ever saw. One must become half-Catholic to enter fully into the glories of Italian art—religion with us is a cold, reluctant duty. We acknowledge God, but fear to love him. We are afraid of any thing that fit our minds for devotion—we make religion a duty, not an affection—will when the formality of worship is over, we have done. The true spirit, superstition, devotion, whatever you will—was in the heart of the Italian artist—it oozed out at the end of his pencil, bathing his work in the beauty of holiness."

Mr. Beckford then went over the lines, suggesting two verbal alterations. There was a line

Into a shapeless mass of quivering pain,

"Good," said he, "of one broken on the wheel."

There was also a quotation from Milton,

Dark with excessive bright.

He began the passage of Milton in which the quotation is found, repeating by heart twenty or thirty lines of the "Paradise Lost."

"How gloriously sublime he is—Michael Angelo and Raffaelle together."

In this skippish way, passing from subject to subject, he observed that he had called upon the Duchess-dowager of Sutherland, an acquaintance of long standing—he had few left.

"Peel went out just as I arrived. Sir Robert wants something to do, I suppose, to pass his time, now he is out of office. Whether he was trying to inoculate the duchess with his anti-ministerial feelings I do not know, but she seemed very apprehensive about property being endangered in the existing state of things. I told her I had no such alarm. There was no danger to be feared for property until the finances became deranged from the taxes not being sustainable—until the interest to meet the debts of George III. could not be provided. All who have any thing to lose must become discontented before property is in hazard, except in a temporary riot—there will be many warnings—every body now has some property to lose. I was in France during the Revolution—that began with disorganized finances — Neckar would have arranged all, but the jealousies of party prevented—they turned out Neckar, and cut their own throats."

"You knew his daughter, I presume?"

"Before her marriage, in her father's time. Did you know her when you were living in Paris?"

"I was introduced to her in Argyle-street here, in 1814 or 1815. I called the first time early, wishing to see her alone. Mademoiselle de Staël told me her mother was never up until two o'clock—it was then nearly three."

"That was her custom. I knew her at Coppet, a lovely place near Geneva, long, very long ago. She preferred the *Chaussée d'Antin*—woman in her inclinations, she thought like a man—wrote like a man—luxuriated in the stagnant vapours of a large capital, where she played the owl—she loved to display herself by wax-light. She would have exchanged her fame for beauty—how womanish! Her figure was good—I remember her a very symmetrical young lady, who might have sat, as the Princess Borghese did, to Canova, and made a respectable statue."

"She told Lord Boringdon, on his inviting her to his country house, in December, that she was engaged every day until the ninth of April—that she might avoid a country visit."

"Exactly, like her. Pray, do you know Hook, the novelist?"

I replied in the affirmative.

"His plots are not very original, nor does he display much thought; but he relates his stories wonderfully well, and introduces his minor incidents with great judgment and effect. I could not get him out of my head yesterday. He brings a pretended surveyor of a railroad to the owner of a pet house, telling him he is come to take bearings for a railroad, which is to proceed right through his property. The alarm he causes is ludicrous and well-sustained. Such incidents seem to be his forte—they say he is an *improvvisante?*"

"Like an Italian; with a rugged material in our language, rendering the task more difficult—his skill in that way is wonderful—he has his joke, good or bad, upon every thing."

"A hazardous gift," observed Mr. Beckford, "even at the convivial hour. Wits are great diners—dining much in company ruins health. When the stomach goes, the man dies—take care of dinners."

A volume of Saurin's sermons was on the table—the name he pronounced Soree. Mr. Beckford preferred Saurin's to all others.

"To Massillon's?" I asked.

"To all others, French or English—Massillon takes higher flights, he preached before crowned heads as he would do before ordinary people — the sermons of neither were like silken and scented discourses. I have had a correspondence with a dissenting minister, the Rev. Mr. Jay, upon the badness of the psalms and hymns used in worship, considered as poetical compositions. Some may think this a matter of no moment. One of the popes said it was blasphemous to submit the word of God to the rules of grammatical composition—God should have the best that can be offered in relation to his worship—church and chapel make sad work of their psalmody."

He made no further mention of this subject, which must have been curiously treated if he had gone into it at length. He wrote poetry* with

* The following beautiful lines, entitled "A Prayer," are proof of this. They were published in another work many years ago.

Like the low murmur of the secret stream,
  Which through dark alders winds its shaded way,
My suppliant voice is heard: ah, do not deem
  That on vain toys I throw my life away!

great excellence, his mind was eminently poetical — he had profound ideas upon the wisdom and goodness of the Supreme Being; these he sometimes mingled with his enjoyments of picturesque nature, his love of which was intense, seeing all with a poet's eyes—the wilder, the more attractive.

"I have sometimes felt unable to separate myself without great difficulty from certain spots that fixed my attention. Night has found me in my noonday resting-place, too far sometimes from the halting-place of my attendants. Carriage, friends, servants, if with me, I have suffered to proceed, and feeling the inclination irresistible, have mounted an attendant's horse, and rode, my heart exulting, into some romantic mountain gorge, got off, flung myself upon a bed of verdure on the banks of a sparkling stream, and wished the moments I spent there, and the sensations I experienced, to be eternal—sensations with which, I suppose, the couple in Paradise filled their measure of happiness. To me, nothing can surpass in attraction, a hillock in a vineyard at sunset—a peasant's vineyard among the Appenines near a gushing stream of water. I can recall such a spot to my recollection at this moment where I fell into a reverie. I was roused by a great bird flapping his broad sail-like wings over my head—sounds are very distinctly heard from a great distance in mountain solitudes, where the air is rare and transparent. I looked up and was instantly reminded of the devil's wings, so sail-like in expansion:

l'ali
Che 'n guisa hà pur di due gran vele aperte.

The clothing of the Appenines has a thousand gradations of colour; vegetation rises to a great height. The hues of nature made the artists of Italy colourists."

"But the greatest colourists were of Venice, the least picturesque part of Italy—was it not so?"

"You have not seen Venice. Every tint beneath that sky is dipped in heaven. Nothing can surpass the gorgeous magnificence of the light there at certain times—the pallid green at night's approach is peculiar. The sea is of intense azure, dotted with golden islets. If there are not vales and mountains, there is still an infinite diversity of colour. The eyes of a Venetian would call the sea at Dover pale blue, on our finest summer's day—hence we sometimes think the sky in Italian paintings too blue."

I was going into Staffordshire. Mr. Beckford desired me to see the woods of Ilam on the borders of Derby.* Had I seen the mountains of

---

In the recesses of the forest vale,
On the wild mountain, on the verdant sod,
Where the fresh breezes of the morn prevail,
I wander lonely, communing with God.

When the faint sickness of a wounded heart
Creeps in cold shudderings through my sinking frame,
I turn to Thee—that holy peace impart
Which soothes the invokers of thy awful name!

O all-pervading Spirit!—sacred beam!
Parent of life and light!—Eternal Power!
Grant me, though obvious clouds, one transient gleam
Of Thy bright essence in my dying hour!

* I did so, and found the scenery very fine. Out of the way as that district is, it shows how little of home scenery had escaped Mr. Beckford's observation.

North Wales? I had scaled both Snowdon and Cader Idris—I had clambered the Dôle. There was no such panorama besides on earth as that of the Dôle—it was the finest thing mortal vision could comprehend. That vast semicircle—the Dôle the centre—the whole Alps the concave. The intervening field so vast and varied. He had never been able to discover the peak of Snowdon for clouds—he could live very comfortably at the foot of a Welsh mountain, in a cottage, with his books and the indulgence of a horse to range through the wild, craggy vallies. He wondered he had not gone from Fonthill to some of the mountain districts. I asked if the scenery of the rock of Lisbon was sublime. It was grandly beautiful.

"You are not aware, perhaps, that I offered my services to the government, at a critical moment, as an envoy to the court of Lisbon. My acquaintance with the Prince Regent, and my intimacy with the Marialva family, adapted me for such a post. It came to nothing; but I think I could have done the country some service. In the Marialva villa at Cintra, where I passed so many delightful hours, the celebrated convention was signed, for which Sir Arthur Wellesley then, was so much censured."

I inquired about a family at Lisbon—the Torres family, one of whom went out archbishop to Rio, his nephew I had known at the time the court fled to the Brazils. The name was familiar to Mr. Beckford, but he did not know which of them was appointed subsequently to the archbishopric. I told him that I had heard the house at his quinta was standing, and some of the plate-glass still left in the windows, but that the plough worked up to the door of his deserted villa, over the ground where his trees, shrubs, and flowers, had luxuriously flourished.

"Likely enough," he remarked; "but my friends are all dead—no matter—it is the course of destiny—you remember where I quote:

> neque harum, quas celis arborum
> Te præter invisus cupressos
> Ulla brevem dominum sequetur!

This touching allusion is exemplified—the proud, rich, gifted man—the spoiled son of fortune—the eccentric and philosophic—who quitted his palace with an indifference worthy of antiquity, declaring he could exchange it for a cottage without a pang, met his death as tranquilly as might be expected from his intellectual and reflective constitution. His temperance and activity prolonged his life to eighty-four in full possession of his faculties—to the last busied in his customary manner. He was occupied with books even after his indisposition commenced—his wonderful vision gratified the love of art that age did not appear to diminish—fortunate in the extent of his acquirements, his enjoyments were proportionably multiplied — fortunate in surviving detraction. He struggled manfully at first against the fever which carried him off, arising from a cold caught after overwalking himself in the late chill easterly wind. When he saw that the struggle was vain, not before, and that the last of life was approaching, he wrote to his affectionate daughter in town, his last laconic note, "Come—quick!—quick!" and expired a day or two after the duchess's arrival, with perfect resignation so tranquilly that his passing moment was hardly perceptible.

THE TOWER OF THE CALIPH.

[In the June number of the *New Monthly*, was a short notice of the Tower erected on Lansdown, by the Author of "Vathek." As the Tower has been recently renovated, a more particular description of its existing state may not be found uninteresting.]

Being at Bath, the weather insufferably hot, I rose early after a feverish slumber, and mounted Lansdown Hill, at the foot of which I had taken up my quarters. The atmosphere on the hill-top was deliciously fresh. Not a cloud sullied the blue serene; the sun had attained but a trifling elevation; the western shadows were projected, long and gaunt, from tower and tree; the herbage glistened with the dew, and the lark, mounting with hurried wing, trilled its own peculiar warble impetuously gleesome. On the floor of mist in the ravines far below, the sunbeams glanced obliquely and faintly, concealing underneath its fleecy surface many a hallowed fane and stately edifice. Distant summits peered above the mist in the valleys; those furthest off tinged with faint purple. The site of many an unseen cot was discoverable by the gray smoke of its early fire, curling in graceful wreaths before dark, deep masses of foliage, that in tufted patches ornamented an almost unrivalled landscape. The low of cattle, betokening pasturages near, struck upon the ear, recalling other scenes and other days, the symptoms of commencing reverie. On a sudden the resonance of a church-bell announced the hour of seven. I began to descend towards the population beneath, that had not yet made itself visible. Around me the bees more wakeful were humming in beguilement of their tiny toils, and the butterflies, all gaiety of plumage, emulated the belles not far off in the rainbow-hued robes, which the last had doffed from the ball of the previous night, and had not yet resumed.

On coming to a mass of lofty buildings in my descent, behind which a road pointed to the right, that might lead into the city by another route than I had before traversed, I turned aside. After following the new direction for some distance between stone walls, an archway appeared on the left, connecting two large houses. Through the opening thus afforded, still tinged with the gray vapour of the morning, was seen uprising the most beautiful of British cities. There trees, gardens, towers, and architectural magnificence, mingled in surpassing beauty, backed by abrupt eminences, studded with villas, and dotted with groves worthy of Arcady.

Opposite the arch, a road pointed upwards between walls, over which fruit hung thickly clustering. Some little way further on, a door wide open disclosed extensive gardens. On the north side stretched double walls, one above another. Parallel with the highest, ran a walk leading to an antique gateway, embattled, machicolated, and nearly buried in trees. I never saw such a prodigality of fruitage of every variety. The walls were in a blush with the warm tints of the peach and other wall-fruit, glowing freshly in the bright morning sun. I was tempted to enter, expecting to find some one to whom, apologising for my intrusion, I might inquire who was the owner of so prolific a spot. No one appeared—all was silence. I walked along the principal path, overlaid with glittering quartz. Here were long espaliers that groaned beneath their precious products of apple and pear, there huge pendent plums of all colours and sizes. The place seemed to be under the spell of enchantment. I lingered within the charmed precincts, but no creature appeared to warn or welcome. In front a flight of steps led to a terrace. These I mounted, traversed a terrace almost Italian in appearance, and reached the embattled gate, which I found unlocked, pushed gently open, passed out, and closed—the work of a moment. I was not displeased at finding myself beyond the garden on which I had trespassed. I now trod a field of some extent, bordered by hedgerows of thorn, cut in irregular clumps, apparently to avoid the sameness of stiff clipping in the monotonous mode customary. I was on the ascent of the hill, the higher side of the field being bounded by palisades, beyond which a public path crossed, a second row of palisades intervened, and then another enclosure appeared, which I entered, and afterwards another. An irresistible desire to explore the domain on which I had so trespassed, spurred me forward. It was better to be met in an open field by the owner, than in a walled garden filled with choice fruit. I did not fear being mistaken for a Nebuchadnezzar, and punished for the theft of animal sustenance—the garden was a different thing; a repository of every species of fruit that could lead to temptation, might give well-grounded suspicion of furtive intention.

I next arrived at a plantation, having a turf-walk curving along the hill-side. At short intervals, on each hand, beds of thyme, marjoram, and all kinds of scented and aromatic herbs were introduced, as if they had sprung up naturally, perfuming the air with their sweets. Rude seats invited to a notice of manifold variations in the prospect, generally formed of the block section of a felled tree. In one place, where there was an elbow in the road, on turning suddenly round, I beheld one of the most beautiful views that could delight human sight. The elevation was considerable. Far beneath, in snaky curves, a bright stream shone, like liquid silver, tower, hamlet, grove, meadow, hill, mansion, and villa, were seen under every variety of aspect, until blending in the offskip, they composed the indistinct distance. I flung myself supinely upon a bed of camomile, that exuded its well known aromatic perfume. A gentle breeze had arisen, tempering the sun's heat, and keeping the distant promontories in haze. I lingered on the spot, comforting myself that if seen by some surly gamekeeper, I might still escape with no other injury than the infliction upon the ear of some vulgar adjuration. I had neither gun nor snare in my possession. These reflections were of no moment, for no intruder upon my intrusion manifested himself.

I now came upon an open space of ground, covered with grass-grown mounds, where all was as solitary as if it were the site of a buried city. From hence there was no prospect, the irregular sod being on one hand, and the front view bounded by plantations. On the left, in a wall of rock, yawned cavernous excavations that had been made at some remote time, either for the excavation of stone, which in the oolite strata is always taken with more facility in the horizontal than the perpendicular direction, or to form habitations for our rude forefathers. Fires had blackened each yawning interior, and given them a grim sombre aspect. Indeed, they might have been taken for deserted tombs, by no great stretch of fancy, in a spot so full of solitary associations, where all was designedly left to the rough tutorship of nature. There was something strange and mystical about the appearance of the place. The sky above, and desolation beneath, imparted to the spirit the idea of an utter separation from the rest of the species.

Proceeding along the left boundary of this rude spot, seemingly shut out from the world, a gate met my view, leading into a plantation, and passing through, a little way on, a wall with a small door, crossed the path. I had gone on so far prosperously; it was not amiss to tempt the end of the adventure which seems now of "the stuff that dreams are made of." I lifted the latch and entered. What was my surprise—my amazement at the transition from the savage to the cultivated—from the deformed to the beautiful! I found myself at the entrance to a garden of a thousand flowers—a garden glowing with roses in full bloom, through the centre of which the path led. On both sides the loveliest flowers were blooming, and sending up their odours even to faintness from the intensity of their perfume. They thickened and multiplied as I advanced along an enchanted spot, shut in on all sides, breathing the gales of Araby the Blest. Never did I behold flowers in such profusion—the gardens of Gul could but have rivalled them. Yet no neat parterres, no clipped borders were to be seen. Every species of rose grew at random, intermingled with others of the floral race in prodigality of loveliness. Still I continued to advance, and still neither the variety nor the quantity appeared to diminish. At length I saw before me a house evidently Italianised. Three arched and narrow windows were seen over an arch yet larger, spanning the path. There was a foreign and classical air thus given to the building impossible to be mistaken. Here and there, towards the boundary of this delightful floral assemblage, as if in the way of contrast, broad and green-leafed fig-trees, set off by their density of colour, the rainbow-hued tints of the flowers that grew on every side in such lavish profusion. Passing under the arch already mentioned, the garden was again continued as brilliant as before. Rich perfumes arose from every side. The gorgeous assemblage of flowers, scattered or clumped in bouquets of surpassing beauty, backed by foliage the most verdant, glowing and deepening their many-coloured hues, fixed the sight irresistibly upon their magnificence of colour. The disposition of this garden bore no appearance of art—no formality. The path through such a wilderness of sweets terminated in a dark grotto, rather abruptly descending, having on the right of the entrance a small pool of water that nourished aquatic plants.

In a moment the scene altered from the most beautiful of floral assemblages to the subdued light within a subterranean excavation—a change succeeded in another moment by the stranger's emerging, after a short passage through the grotto, upon a surface bearing no sort of resemblance to that which had preceded. On the right appeared a stone wall, at the foot of which was planted a variety of odoriferous shrubs in a border, bounded by a walk of no great breadth. Outside this an extensive field, covered with short mountain turf, presented itself, on which a few sheep were browsing. These were kept from trespassing on the border by a rough wooden fence. Glancing in a western direction across the turf, unrelieved by a single flower, the eye first became sensible of its elevation on table land, far above the neighbouring hills, the summits of which were seen undulating into the far distance—sinking into the gray tint so distinctive of intervening space.

But what was in front across the sward, at the distance of a few hundred yards ?—what but a beautiful shrubbery, the mass in every shade of green, here and there interspersed with flower or berry-bearing trees. Over the irregular line of verdure thus discovered, there rose a lofty tower of a square form, crowned with a handsome and classical ornament, the choragic monument of Lysicrates at Athens, placed one hundred and twenty feet in the air—the exquisite, well-proportioned columns and domed roof appearing to wonderful advantage.

Beneath this graceful ornament was a square room, immediately resting on the tower summit, like a statue upon a column. Three arched windows of plate-glass lighted each face. Beneath, about half the body of the tower was visible, peering upwards amid the surrounding foliage. Shortly, on approaching near the shrubbery, the tower that produced an effect so magical, as to attract the vision from every other object, wholly disappeared. I was too much delighted to think of retracing my footsteps. A paradise opened before me in the shrubbery, as with solitary step and curious eye I entered its enchanting wilderness of vegetative life. A winding path, here bounded by flowering shrubs, or bushes of rare growth, there by rose-trees, beyond which were bushes of various kinds, or flowering shrubs—sometimes the uniformity broken by little pools of water, fringed with curious plants, or rustic seats, or dark, dim overshadowing umbrage. Graceful and fragrant branches pendent, down sometimes to the long tangled grass suffered to spring wildly in apparent neglect of art, curved their novel leafage on either hand. A patch of emerald turf intervened, through which uprose the wild yellow tulip, close to lilies and violets, that appeared to owe their existence on that spot to a generous accident of nature. Every quarter of the globe seemed to have been ransacked in order to extend the variety of the vegetative kingdom flourishing here. Rock roses of the sunny south were abundant. The Alpine schistus bordered upon bushes of sweetbriar in native wildness. The libertine honeysuckle, spread its slender branches, entwining amidst and over all, in great luxuriance of flower and strength of odour. The pinus arborea assumed the character of a tree. Of the pine genus there were rare specimens; the spots selected for the growth of the coniferæ, being, when necessary, carefully sheltered or secluded. The Brazils, the Himalaya, Mexico, and Scotland, alike contributed to adorn this delightful and sequestered shrubbery, in which too patches of dark yew might be seen waving their gloomy boughs in melancholy stateliness. Advantage was taken of every nook where ornament could be introduced, without disturbing the broader masses, or exhibiting marks of care or cultivation, evidently the effect of consummate taste united with experienced judgment. There was a repose and harmony over all bewitchingly attractive.

I lingered as if I was spell-bound in some magic garden of the warm East—some dreamy spot that Arabian imaginativeness had created for the hero of one of those immortal stories, which none but the fancies of those who revel in the glories of happy climes can embody. All was bud and blossom in luxuriant assemblage, appearing at a distance one extended mass of varied and brilliant colour, revelling in the full glare of the sunbeams. In shady places, among stones, and where the roughness of the ground demanded concealment, there grew many varieties of fern. In one spot, the Osmandi Regale waved its palmy foliage over beds of antirrhinum, and carpets of wild thyme alternated with common turf. Many of the trees and shrubs presented an aspect completely novel in their forms and foliage, imparting a foreign appearance to the umbrage. Placing myself upon a stone seat, I began to imagine myself in a distant land—in some Damascene garden, especially as my solitude continued unbroken, except by the sweet harmony of an infinite variety of birds, that made the thickets a favourite retreat, if their mellifluous notes were any criterion of their regard for the locality. A thrush seemed to outdo the utmost efforts of his brother tenants of the air, making the charming spot vocal with the richest tones of untaught music.

I continued my walk amid hope, fear, and delight, each alternately president in my mind. I wound along the paths; I imagined a hundred strange day-dreams; continually halting at new beauties of vegetative growth. I could not help thinking that a few of the Easterns in their romantic costume would have heightened the illusion. The sunny warmth, the odours on every side, the silence, the deep shadows, and the air of adventure withal, prepared the mind for orientalism and magic. Nor was this impression diminished when coming suddenly upon an open space, silent, solitary, yet green and beautiful, as a place of death should ever be, I found, in a leafy recess on one side, a sarcophagus of rose-coloured granite. This receptacle of the dead was eight or nine feet long, nearly six high, and polished up to the brilliancy of a looking-glass. "Doubtless the tomb of the genius of the place," thought I, "if a genius may die." How beautiful a bed of repose in so elevated a spot! Amid such a scene, if human ashes are watched by the shadowy principle that once animated them with the power of memory and judgment, it must be the most pleasant of duties, until time has wrought manifold transmutations into unrecognisable atoms, when the spirit, no longer able to trace its ancient habitation, wings its final flight to other orbs. Here was a sepulchre worthy the proudest monarch—fit to consume the fleshless forms of the pre-adamite kings. I now passed on, and had not proceeded many paces, clearing the shrubbery a few yards, when full before me rose the beautiful tower of which I have already spoken. The upper part I have already described. The lower half sprung from the ground with two sides joined to a square edifice of a couple of stories in height, all constructed of mellow-coloured freestone. The proportions were highly symmetrical. The windows, narrow and circular headed, were each composed of an entire piece of plate-glass.

Proceeding towards the entrance of the building, and ascending two or three steps, I found myself in a sort of entrance-hall. It was a narrow apartment, having a door on the left leading into a room in which the prevalent colour was scarlet. A second door, with arched panels of plate-glass, led to the stairs. In this, the hall of entrance, in a small recess on the right hand, stood a noble pillar-table of Sienna marble. This table bore three Etruscan vases of the more remote fabric, and behind them was a mirror in three compartments, having semicircular tops, answering in form to the windows elsewhere. The ceiling border of wainscot was ornamented with gilt cornices. The parallel rafters or beams, had their intermediate ceilings decorated with red panelling, at once tasteful and magnificent. Suspended glazed cabinets bore many articles, precious and rare, arranged with consummate taste. Agreeable combinations seemed to have been carefully studied, while at the same time instruction was conveyed to the beholder, by the illustration of objects through their regular approximation in a proper series. Of these the Etruscan vases, already mentioned, formed one. A vase here, almost unique, bore over a ground powdered with gold, the representation of a black and bearded Bacchus.

I observed several antiquities in metal; among them a bronze bust of Caligula, having silver eyes. This was once the property of Horace Walpole, and came from Strawberry Hill. It was found in Herculaneum. There can be little doubt that this bust bore a likeness of the emperor—the workmanship was exquisite. It was once the property of Prince Elbœuf, among whose effects it was sold at Florence.

The apartment on the right of the entrance-hall produced a singular effect upon my mind. It overwhelmed me with its expression of elegance and comfort, its feeling of unequivocal enjoyment. Translated by a few steps from a region of natural beauty, to one altogether artificial, one of refinement and classical taste, nothing was lost by the contrast. The nature of the objects for which the exchange was made, being so different, there was no depreciating comparison. A rich and almost dazzling effect arose from the predominance of scarlet in every thing attaching to this room. The walls, hangings, full draperies, carpet were of this colour and black. The arrangement was admirable. Every thing, to the minutest bit of pearl, engraved crystal, japan work, or statuary being precisely in the best possible place. The effect of all thus regulated, seemed to be the generation of a fear of disarrangement—a desire to leave every thing unhandled and sacred, like the regalia of the altar in a place of catholic worship. The ornaments, appeared under a spell, which the vulgar habit of touch would dissolve, disarming the coarse propensity of its power of action.

Over the mantel-piece was a picture by the noted Hondekoeter, the principal object in which was a splendid game-cock in the full glory of his plumage, bright and glossy as nature itself, and of the purest scarlet. It was as if every thing in the room was coloured after this beautiful creature into one general harmony of hue. Between the beams of the ceiling the panel work was scarlet, with a relief of purple and gold. Yet there was nothing tawdry; all was kept down and subdued into a uniform glow of overpowering elegance, which in no one instance appeared to have been trespassed upon. The fire-place was composed of Brocatelli marble. Under a window opposite was a large table of Egyptian granite, bearing an ivory vase lined with crystal, and filled with the richest and freshest flowers, from among which, long pendant sprays of jessamine, sweetbriar, and wild rose, set off by their dark green hues, the richer colours with which they were intermingled, filling the room with the freshest fragrance.

On the chimney-piece were two lizard bottles of the rarest kind, sea-green in colour. I observed some oriental cups, with ornaments on a scarlet ground, mostly of gold, with which indeed they were lined. Some of the enamels were wonderfully well executed, among them were large dishes of the most costly workmanship. Vases of Italian porphyry, verte antique, Egyptian granite, and Sienna marble, here met the view, with carved oak coffers containing specimens of rare japan, elaborately inlaid with coral and pure gold. There was also a tripod under the western window, supporting a slab of Lumachelle from the Himalaya mountains. There was no confusion from the too great multiplication of similar objects—there was enough, and no more. Nothing could be more judicious and tasteful than the arrangement—nothing more approaching the faultless.

Among the pictures were a very pleasing landscape by John Both—an admirable portrait of a Doge of Venice, by Giovanni Bellini—a landscape, by Cemaroli—the Thistle, a landscape, by Wynants—the Triumph of the Gods, by Franken—the Tower of Babel, and a Coronation by West.

Over the mantel-piece hung two fine enamels, and a Greek legendary painting of great antiquity, divided into three compartments. In addition to these was a small Breughal of beautiful execution.

The door leading to the stairs served as an entrance to all the other parts of the tower. Ascending to the upper floor, my eye was struck in the centre of the well formed by the winding stairs, with a noble vase of polished granite, having bronze ornamented cornices, and four lions' heads protruding from as many openings or cells in the base. Large, elegant, and singularly well placed, this was a very striking object both as a specimen of art and a beautiful ornament.

A door on the left hand conducted me into a room hung with crimson. The lower room, so prodigal of beauty, was outdone here. Nothing could be more chastely elegant, more soberly rich. The hangings, draperies, carpets, and walls, were of rich crimson. The ceiling purple, crimson and gold panelling. Against the southern side stood an ebony cabinet of exquisite workmanship, the top a precious slab of green porphyry. This cabinet contained some specimens of rare japan. A coffer here once belonged to the noted Cardinal Mazarin; it was placed upon a table of Florentine mosaic, exceedingly beautiful. I observed that all the tables were of valuable Italian marbles, made after the most classical designs. Several of the candelabra were of polished granite. On every side were vases of rare china, jasper, calcedony, agate, cornelian, brocatelli, and similar rare or curious substances, many exquisitely formed, and sculptured elaborately. Here, too, were hanging cabinets, containing books and vases. Among these, of unparalleled rarity, was a curious Venetian vase of glass, of considerable antiquity. It was enamelled and gilt with figures of knights and combats of chivalry, exciting surprise at the freshness and splendour of its illuminations. Artists must have examined it with wonder. The legend it represented was incomprehensible to the unlearned, and a puzzle to those who might hereafter attempt to explain the subject. The bare preservation of such a relic, considering the fragile material of which it was made, did not seem the least singularity attached to it. The glass appeared thin, and incapable of sustaining even the smallest degree of violence.

There were a pair of candlesticks from the Alhambra, with pyramidical bases, bearing all over their surfaces every kind of arabesque ornament, with an infinity of scrolls and intersecting lines, producing a very rich effect. Another pair of candlesticks here were made of the purest gold, executed by Vuliamy, after a design of Holbein. An enamelled salver, by Jean Cousin, after Raffaelle, representing a feast of the gods, from the Farnesini; above all, the small but celebrated bronze of John of Bologna, representing a Centaur carrying off a female, were among the more striking and precious ornaments of this remarkable room.

A fine St. John, by Murillo; a battle piece, by Bourgonone; the interior of a church, by Antony de L'Orme, the figures by Palamedes; two paintings of Peter Neefs; the interior of a church, by Steinwick; two sweet Italian landscapes, by Herman Swaneveldt, sometimes called the Hermit of Italy, the scholar of Claude le Lorrain; the interior of a palace saloon, by Basan; a head by Albert Durer; Tobit and the Angel, by Elsheimer; and several other choice paintings were here.

A door in one corner of this room led into a closet having a coved ceiling, the window trellised, and the framework gilded. This delightful little retreat was filled with valuable books, beneath which were costly japan articles in cabinets, so as to leave no space unoccupied.

A room adjoining the former, long and narrow, was devoted exclusively to the purpose of a library, and literally lined with books. Here I was tempted to linger for a longer space of time than in the other apartment—it was truly a place in which a man might take up an everlasting rest. The volumes were arranged with great care, so that every advantage was taken of the space. Each book filled its place exactly and closely in the most symmetrical order. Some works bore very expensive binding, many were in white vellum and gold, with appropriate devices to their contents. Others wore the garb of morocco, crimson, green, purple, and even cream-colour, a goodly number being highly embellished. Illuminated missals and psalters of regal costliness were not wanting. Some of these contained miniatures by Julio Clovis, others were gem-clasped, and bound in tortoise-shell, engraved with great care. The subjects of these engravings were miniature landscapes, flowers, and figures, copied from eminent artists, rare, expensive, and beautiful beyond conception. Among them were all that knowledge, influence, and perseverance, in union with wealth, were able to command. Here too were illustrations of the Lord's Prayer, of the Acts of the Apostles, and of the Old Testament, embracing every known published print, and many original drawings by artists of celebrity. Nor were there wanting manuscripts of various kinds, particularly Persian. Chinese printed volumes, in the language of Confucius, oriental tablets, and rarest of all books in Japanese, exceedingly curious in the choicest libraries.

Over the tops of the book-cases were tazzas of precious marbles, with Etruscan vases; some of these last among those most prized from being painted on a white ground. Above all, the ceiling shone conspicuous, in gold, purple, and scarlet, between wainscot beams. This wood, plain and gilded, was used throughout with a neat and uncommonly pleasing effect. The library was approached by a lobby, into which the light was introduced through the roof in a soft, subdued tone, falling upon an antique bronze bust of an individual unknown.

That in so small a space so much of elegance and splendour could be introduced was a matter of surprise. I went from room to room, continually discovering something new. That nothing might be wanting, the *genius loci* had not neglected an apartment devoted to religious uses. Here the light admitted through dim cupolas of ground glass, was remarkably subdued and soft, producing a very solemn effect as it fell upon a full length figure of St. Anthony, with the infant Saviour smiling in his arms, by Rossi. The marble, of a mellow hue, was, by the effect of the restrained light, seen to great advantage. Nothing was wanting to produce the full effect of one of those little chapels seen branching from the dim aisles of a vast Catholic cathedral, but lighted tapers on each side the pedestal of the image. This pedestal was of Sienna marble, standing in a niche pannelled with Egyptian porphyry and mosaic work, having a border of Giallo Antico, and other marbles; it bore the inscription "Dominus Illuminatio mea." That apartments thus fitted up do prepare the mind for the solemn and affecting duties of religion there cannot be the smallest doubt. The mysterious light thus diffused by art scatters all the intruding feelings of levity, and acts continually as a memento that a beseeming spirit must accompany the act of devotion, and that for a few moments at least this world and its associations must give place to the contemplation of one with which the sense is unacquainted, and of which the mind can only image the shadowy outline.

Beneath the cupola were three beautiful semicircular pictures, representing the "Temptation in the Wilderness," "The Annunciation," and "Christ's agony in the Garden," painted by Mr. Willes Maddox, an artist recently from Italy, imbued with a genuine southern feeling for art in its nobler sense. These paintings were the last fixed in this room, denominated "the sanctuary." Besides these there was a Virgin and Child in the style of Raffaelle; the Interior of a Cathedral by Steinwick; three enamels upon sacred subjects and the intombment; and cabinets containing books on sacred literature. Other appropriate articles were placed at the sides of this apartment.

Leaving the sanctuary, and ascending the carpetted stairs of the tower, I came, after climbing a pretty long ascent, into a square room, the drapery of which was orange coloured. The long arched windows of plate glass in each front, disclosed one of the noblest views on which the eye could expatiate. A vast panorama here was only limited by hill summits that undulated far away like the ocean waves. At a vast distance the horizon view terminated in the blue mountains of Wales. In another direction was the sea sparkling and flashing in the sunbeams, here and there carrying a white sail, a mere speck in the far-off part of the landscape. Cities, towns, hamlets, villas, cottages, an almost endless variety of objects, basking in light, or reposing in mild shadow, struck the sight at the first glance with unwonted astonishment. On the north a dreary plain, the scene of many bloody combats, marked by the monument of a fallen chief, stretched away in gloomy monotony. In another direction deep valleys, to the profound of which the eye could not penetrate, offered their sides, decorated with every adjunct of rural beauty for the visual banquet of the beholder. To change from window to window, shifting the scene and returning to where the eye set out, there to repeat the operation, and retire with unfeigned reluctance, was my lot. It is difficult to imagine it was not the same with all who might ever set their feet in a building not less attractive for its artificial beauties than its delightful remoteness from the busy world amid the grandeur of its own solitude. A central staircase from this elevated room, which was denominated the Belvidere with strict appropriateness, led still higher into the lantern of cast iron. Here the openings through the ornamental foliage of the frieze being filled with plate glass, gave a more extensive view than could be obtained in the room beneath, though not with the same convenience of easy seats for careless lounging after the toil of the ascent.

Every thing connected with the edifice on which I had thus trespassed was in the southern taste, strictly Italian. Nothing Oriental or Moorish could be traced in the design. Every thing necessary in the way of use was rendered conducive to ornament. The trellis work of the windows, made of iron, designed to resist the attempts of depredators, was of the most agreeable pattern, and in many cases gilded. The ornaments of ebony, ivory, or metal, the vases, candelabra, carvings, cornices, and the like, were of the purest taste and most correct form. There were no showy gewgaws, no multiplications of ornament or furniture to overdoing. The chairs and couches were generally of ebony, having seats to harmonize with the draperies, some of them ornamented in addition with gilded studs.

Never did human mind plan a more delightful place of study. The books within, the silence around, the very rush of the wind when high, or its soft sighing as it swept by the tower at that great elevation, seemed to solicit thoughtfulness—to explain that it was a place for communing with the deep things of the heart—that there the spirit might almost hear its own whisperings of joy or sorrow—of far-fetched imagining, or revive scenes of bygone times. The garden and shrubbery of this tasteful creation were alike friendly to contemplation, for it had its open and covered walks, its labyrinths of shade and numerous retired seats. Interruption was impossible without scaling walls and fences that were raised along the boundaries of the little paradise, on the sides from whence intrusion could alone be expected. Surely, thought I, it is something to enjoy the labours of great souls in such a spot as this—the least perishable of mortal productions should be tasted where they can be most relished.

I once more entered the library before saying adieu to this scene of enchantment. Taking down a volume in Spanish I began to read in what the author styled "The looking-glass of the soul." Evidently a monkish production, it was still full of matter harrowing up the mind—a mortal in the decay of the grave, conscious of its state and examining its own past frailties. I did not read far. There was something more mild and forgiving about the locality—something impressing me with the belief that the beneficence of the Being that afforded such enjoyment as with every allowance for mortal alloy might be shared here, was not the Being of terror thus represented. I turned to other volumes, that such a solitude could not fail to render productive of more refined associations, tending towards the contemplation of better things than every day existence affords.

I had read but a short time when I heard voices below. I descended into the entrance-hall; a domestic who had the care of the place was conversing with the gardener. "We saw you, though you did not see us; we knew you were one of the very few who might be permitted to trespass so we left you to yourself."

The Tower of the Caliph* stands—but its creator is no more. The bouquets of flowers he daily before his breakfast hour placed in the ground apartment, have faded for ever That tower remains a monument of a mind gifted with acquirements of a rare character and variety; a genius sublime, meditative, retiring, proud, seeking among invisible things those which the visible could not unfold, still acquiring knowledge in the bosom of the solitude so congenial to his temper, even after octogenarian years. The traveller will long regard the beautiful object with delight; the man of letters will renew his wonder at the extent of the founder's acquirement, and the artist will admire the purity of his taste, and the exception to the multitude of the opulent, who lavish wealth upon objects so much more beneath the dignity of humanity.

NERKE.

* A descriptive account of this beautiful building by Mr. English, jun., of Bath, with very beautiful illustrations, made under Mr. Beckford's own inspection, by his *protégé* artist, Mr. W. Maddox, is shortly to make its appearance on a large and handsome scale.

THE

NEW MONTHLY

MAGAZINE

AND

Humorist.

1844.

PART THE THIRD.

LONDON:

HENRY COLBURN, GREAT MARLBOROUGH ST.

SOLD BY ALL BOOKSELLERS.

C. WHITING, BEAUFORT HOUSE, STRAND.

CONVERSATIONS WITH THE LATE W. BECKFORD, ESQ.

CONTRIBUTED BY VARIOUS FRIENDS.

No. III.

It was in the year 1831, and under the following circumstances, that I first had the honour of making the acquaintance of the late W. Beckford, Esq., and which I am proud to say continued until the period of his much lamented demise.

In early youth I showed a disposition for drawing, which was considered by my family to indicate some little promise. It was determined by my father, who had, like Mr. Shandy, his own original and favourite notions, that I should be permitted to follow it as a profession, for, said the good old gentleman, "I hold it to be one of the greatest errors a parent can commit not to let boys have their own way in the choice of a profession. I hold it as my positive opinion," he continued, "that no father is justified in making them shoemakers, when their inclinations prompt them to become cobblers." I had not long returned from Cambridge, where I had made some copies from the pictures in the Fitzwilliam museum, when Mr. ——, the architect of Mr. Beckford, happening to call, and seeing these youthful productions, expressed a wish that this illustrious patron of art should be allowed also to look at them. My father, who had often wondered at this mysterious recluse, readily availed himself of the proposal, and two o'clock the following day was fixed. As this hour approached, the whole house was in commotion, the servants peeping through keyholes, my father preparing a thousand of his most favourite ideas, and myself in such a feverish state of excitement, that my head seemed to be looking out of every window in the house at the same moment. At last two o'clock struck, and, at the very moment, an outrider came galloping to the door, a chariot and postilion came rapidly following after, and before my mother had time to escape from the drawing-room, or my father had advanced to receive him, the author of "Vathek" was vigorously ascending the stairs, ejaculating as he advanced, "Oh! oh! ah!" Mr. —— presented him to my father, and then to the less worthy representative of the family, myself.

His manner of bowing to me was most courteous and elegant, but as he fixed his peculiarly convex yet small piercing gray eyes upon me, I felt as though he would dive into my thoughts, even though it were through the points of my eyelashes. The character of his countenance struck me to be a mixture of the divine Dante, Lorenzo de Medici, and the Mephistophiles of Faust. His voice was agreeable, his manner energetic, and, when he became excited by conversation, and he allowed his imagination full play, knowledge and persuasion, sublime images and sarcasms, came flooding from his lips in such a powerful stream, that you were forcibly carried by it to the sands of admiration, and there left to bask in the splendour of his genius. He usually kept one of his hands over his mouth when in repose, or when looking at any thing; they were well shaped though thickly freckled. He scarcely ever sat down, but kept moving about, suiting his position to the persons he addressed, so as to watch and study them. He adapted his conversation to your powers, and led you imperceptibly to the subjects you were most master of, or on which you were most enthusiastic. To those who gained his esteem he was ever gracious and affable, but where his displeasure was caused it fell like a dead blight. His dress was that of the last century (a little modernised), top-boots, knee-breeches, a green coat, frill, and white neckcloth. Such was the author of "Vathek" as he stood contemplating the copies I had made.

After remaining in the room about five or ten minutes, during which time his eyes darted toward every part with a rapidity peculiar to his microscopic vision, he turned his back upon the copies, and thus addressed me, "Well, well, they are good—vastly good—I like them much;" and with a power of memory almost inconceivable, he commenced pointing out wherein they were successful in imitating the master, and in what they were deficient. The truth of his remarks were so obvious that I asked him if he had recently seen the originals, to which question he replied that he had not seen them since they were in the collection of the Duke of Orleans. "But you are aware," he added, "that the Viscount Fitzwilliam was more famous for his engravings than for his pictures." I then asked him if his lordship was not a man of great taste? Nobody but those who have conversed with or seen the author of "Vathek" can conceive the extraordinary, contemptuous, and mischievous expression his face would assume when his mind was occupied upon a subject uncongenial to his sentiments or his sympathies. He retreated two or three steps back, screwed up his face and frame, and, with a voice ascending to a higher key, replied, "Oh! gracious goodness, no. He was a poor good-natured sort of thing—a hollyhock—but he had an excellent judge, whom he employed to collect for him; the viscount found the money, and Mr. —— the engravings; but whether they were retouched with ink, or pure from the artist's hand, he was incapable of determining." He was much amused by my telling him that Earl ——, then Lord ——, who had seen these copies a few days before, disapproved of Titian's idea of beauty. "Oh—oh—oh, indeed? so I should imagine. I can well suppose that, were I to judge of his lordship's taste by his wife." His visit was but a short one; and whilst descending the stairs, on his way down, he suddenly turned, and asked me if I would like to see the interior of his house on Lansdown Crescent. I immediately asked him when I should come. "The sooner the better," was the reply. "Shall it be to-morrow? Well, then, let it be to-morrow at ten." Before I could give an answer he was again seated in his carriage, and the squire, as he was called by his servants, was out of sight.

For the remainder of that evening my mind was filled with this strange and original being. I could think of nothing else. He had taken absolutely possession of my faculties; in fact he haunted me; there was something so fascinating in his manner, and so amusing in his conversation—such a commingling of all that was impressive, affable, and kind, that, to use one of his own expressions, "I at once believed in him." As he had shown such punctuality when he honoured us with a visit, I felt it incumbent on myself to be equally precise. I accordingly left home at nine o'clock, and reached Lansdown Crescent long before the appointed hour. Mr. Beckford's dwelling, at that period, consisted of two houses, on the opposite sides of an open way leading from the front of the crescent to its rear; these were joined together by an arch being thrown across, of pure proportions and simple structure; the entrance was under the archway, to the right hand. I stood upon the steps of the doorway just as the clock struck, and, with a nervous hand, gently pulled the bell: —I observed there was no knocker, so that his ever active spirit could not be disturbed by a fashionable rat-a-tat-tat, or, the double knock of Mr. Walker the twopenny postman. The chain was unfastened, and the door opened by a servant, who made a respectful bow. His dwarf was standing in the hall—that singular caricature of man whom I had so frequently seen galloping on his little pony to Weston—a strange creature to fascinate the heart of a sweet and lovely girl. How wondrous strange! And yet to those who know the hearts of women, and have observed their fanciful and capricious ways, it is as nothing.

'Twas he who led me to the room in which Mr. Beckford was. The hall was not particularly spacious. On a side-board were a few exotics, pleasing to the eye, and an emblazoned pedigree of the Beckford family was suspended in a frame to the right upon entering the apartment. The dwarf with his huge head and body, moving upon what seemed scarcely to be legs, announced me. I was received with open hands and cordiality, and "Vathek's" master-mind perceiving, as if by instinct, that my feelings were jarred by the appearance of his strange attendant, exclaimed, "Oh, what do you think of him, eh? Oh, he's a strange thing, isn't he?" turning to see whether he was still behind me. Mr. Beckford laughed, and with unearthly voice told me, "He is a Giaour, and feeds upon toadstools."

I looked at him as if I believed in Giaours, for I was passionately fond of the "Arabian Nights." After paying the usual compliments,

"Come," said he, "I will show you something better to look at than that devil-fish," and stopping before the head of St. Catherine—that exquisite gem which is now in the National Gallery—"Behold that—ah! ah! Oh, gracious heavens—is she not beautiful? What a mouth!—look at the corners of that mouth—no impure twistings—all purity; and the eyes—those eyes which seem to be looking into the very countenance of our divine Saviour with such a holy devotion. There—there, now you see what Raphael is!"

The door opened, and another visiter was introduced, who came waddling up to me. This was poor Tiny—a beautiful black-and-tan of the Blenheim breed. The animal seemed to understand perfectly that I was at liberty to be there, for when admiring it, Mr. Beckford looked at the dog, Tiny laid at his feet, as if its affection for the master was so intense that it felt happy merely by a look. Poor Tiny! thy master was not ungrateful for thy many years of devotion: he has collected together thy bones, and saved thy flesh, and from the destructive winds secure has placed them in a tomb or ark on Lansdown's summit, where ever green shrubs their shadows cast, and "Vathek's" tower darts its proud head unto the floating clouds, and where once stood that granite shell, of large Egyptian form, thy master fashioned for himself.

We again turned to the picture of Raphael.

"It is," said he, "one of the very sweetest heads Raphael ever painted. I know of none so beautiful, except in his picture of the 'Perlaa.' But the finest of all Raphael's productions is the 'Spasimo,' which is in the Escurial."

"What," inquired I, "finer than the 'Transfiguration?'"

"Yes, than as we know the 'Transfiguration,' for I saw it at Paris with a swarm of picture-cleaners (those skinners of pictures), cleaning and scraping, and making spots over it like a group of bluebottle-flies; besides, there was a hole in the centre which was filled up. The Redeemer is very fine, but infinitely inferior to our Lord, as portrayed in the 'Spasimo,' who is bowed down to the earth by the weight of his cross and his sufferings, but in the expression of whom, Raphael has made visible an inward satisfaction struggling over pain, that he is yet to save the world."

During the whole time that I was looking at this picture, which was hung—a line picture, as the aristocracy of the Royal Academy would call it—the light coming in from the left, and beneath which was placed a glass containing some three or five delicate and odoriferous flowers—he went on talking and describing its beauties; then opening the glass before it, he made me look close, to examine Raphael's method of pencilling. What with the flowers, and a sort of spicy perfume which seemed to come forth as he unlocked it, I observed that one might imagine she breathed, and that her breath was like sweet herbs and cinnamon.

He retreated—looked at me—rubbed his fore finger and thumb together, and said, "Ah—ah—good—so you might—I see you appreciate these sort of things."

The next picture we looked at was a Claude Lorraine, which hung above, to the right of the Raphael, and between two Vernets. The subject of the Claude, was "Christ appearing to Mary Magdalene in the Garden," and which has been since sold.

"Oh," he said, "you don't like that—quite right, it is a vile composition, and except for that peculiar and happy hue, like the bloom on a fresh-gathered plum, so exclusively Claude's, and which you find here purer than I ever saw it before, I would not keep the picture an hour."

I then called his attention to the "Mulino," in the National Gallery.

"It is fine," he replied, "but that execrable Seguier has scrubbed away its bloom and virginity. I have an advantage though over you," he said, "for my sight is so acute, that I can see deeper into the paint than you can, and therefore can well imagine what it must have been."

I then pointed to one of the Vernets.

"Ah! clever—yes, yes, it's clever. I hang them there to show the difference of the schools. You have pasticcio and French broth at the same time."

The "Garafolo," now in the National Gallery, was likewise hung in this room. On the opposite side was his famous Gaspar Poussin, under which hung the well-known picture, called the Berghem gem (since sold), a very sweet little bit by Wilson, and some smaller ones by Dutch masters; to the left of these was the fire-place, by the side of which was a basket filled with fir-cone tops. To the left of the fire-place hung, what was decidedly the favourite picture of all his picked collection. I never during the many—many happy hours I have spent in this room, listening to his conversation, historical and family anecdotes, or to his reading autograph letters, correspondences with his daughter, the Duchess of Hamilton, works yet unpublished, such as his "Liber Veritatis," "Episodes of Vathek," &c.,—I never left this room without our mutually admiring this picture by West, the subject of which was "Lear." I would defy the determined hostility and bitterness even of a Peter Pindar not to have been moved with this splendid monarch, "Every inch a king," braving the tempest, wretched, and old, and mad with faithful, anxious watching—Kent close to his side—and Tom—mad Tom—crouched up in the corner cold, "Poor Tom's a cold." Whilst looking at it, "See," said Mr. Beckford, "see how his nostril is inflated, like an Arab in a thunder-storm. I solemnly declare the figure of Lear is as fine as the 'Laocoon,' and the tone is as fine as fine can be. Who could suppose that the genius who had conceived and executed this, could have painted such a wretched and paralytic daub as his picture of 'The Sick brought before Christ,' in the National Gallery. Oh, gracious God! he must have been inspired when he painted this—there's drama, expression, drawing, every thing. Ah! ah! you like that—I see you do, and you are quite right."

I am certain the author of "Vathek" knew perfectly well what was passing in your mind. He has often said to me, "Men's faces are a sort of alphabet to me. I can read their minds as easily as I can read a book."

It was useless to say you liked a thing if you did not; for if you did he would talk at you till he made you perfectly uncomfortable. He was a great lover of truth, proud and determined. To gain his esteem, manliness and straightforwardness, with modesty, were the surest way. At the end of this room was his piano, behind which fell red drapery in large full folds; a Japanese screen stretched from this into the room, so as to exclude all draughts. Over a doorway, to the right of the piano, which led you into another apartment, was a fine specimen of Canaletti. He laughed heartily, at least for him—for there was something very uncommon in his laugh; it consisted more of a succession of pleased exclamations, something of a mental rather than physical operation—on my telling him the anecdote of our famous Etty (for whom he had the greatest admiration), that when at Venice it is reported that he fell into a canal, since which the wits of the Royal Academy say that he was baptised at Venice, and his name is now Canal Etty.

A table at the window, on which were a gold inkstand and gold candlesticks, and a circular one in the centre of the room, at which many a book has been read, and on the fly leaves of which many a bitter thing has been written, were the most conspicuous things in the room he chiefly made use of. Our conversation then returned to West. Mr. Beckford had spent much of his time in his painting-room, and was there one day when Nollekins, the sculptor, came in, after taking a *post mortem* cast of William Pitt's head.

"Gracious God! I shall never forget," said Mr. Beckford, "his placing it on the table, and saying, as he uncovered it, 'It is the head of a fiend, and not a man.' From my having been brought up chiefly at Lord Chatham's, and my associations with the family, it made a strong impression upon me, for Nollekens, merely spoke as a devotee in his profession, not as a political partisan."

As this was touching upon statesmen, I asked his opinion upon some of the most prominent ones then living—more especially concerning one who has since been so anomalously kept in a very prominent position.

"Oh," said Mr. Beckford, "George IV. said every thing of him that can be said. D—n him! I hate him! he is such a strip of calico."

What association of ideas touched upon "Vathek's" mind in talking of Sir Robert ——, George IV., and calicoes, I cannot guess; but he then asked me if I had ever seen West's picture of "Death and the Pale Horse." I answered in the negative.

"I'm sorry for that," and then trotting off, he disappeared for a minute, and came returning with some papers in his hand. He told me to sit down, and taking a chair, placed himself so as the light might fall full upon what he held. Tiny imitated the movements of its master, and betook itself to its cushion on the sofa.

"Oh, let me see—ah, ah—yes, here—here is something very fine!"

Mr. Beckford had a peculiar method of agitating your curiosity. He has often made me feel so impatient to see what he has had in his hands, that it was with difficulty I could refrain from snatching it out of them.

"Look—look—here it is—ah, ah—" and he would show me the outside, with some mark or memorandum upon the cover, and then he would dart off and tell me the history of it, to whom it belonged, and how he came possessed of it, and where it was found, and how it was found, and by whom it was found, and a history of all the people's families in whose possession it had ever been; so that by the time you did see it, your interest was wound up to the highest pitch. Was all this study, or was it the impulses of a quick and rapid imagination, carried from thing to thing by the association of ideas? This is a question I have frequently asked myself.

The paper which he held in his hand, was an engraving by Mark Antonio, of the "Witch" of Michael Angelo; it was the first time I had ever seen an impression of this rare production, and Mr. Beckford took good care that I should not easily forget it, for he descanted as eloquently upon this hag riding on the skeleton of some strange infernal beast, as she is greedily licking up fire from a bowl, as he had previously poured forth his hymn of praise to the beauties of St. Catherine—showing that his soul was equally capable of strong emotions, when it was either touched by the sublime, the beautiful, or the terrible. He urged on me the necessity of carefully studying the engravings of Mark Antonio wherever I had an opportunity; "It is here," he said, "that we can find Raphael pure —for even where his pictures have been saved from the scarifying of picture cleaners—still the varnish has been laid on coat after coat, or the dirt eaten in so as to much impair the delicate little touches—and it is these which give that perfection to his works. The greater number of his pictures were commenced by his pupils, especially by Julio Romano; Raphael then came and put the finishing touches; but if pearl-ashes, vinegar, and spirits of wine are employed, Raphael is quacked to death, and Julio Romano peeps into the world half born."

Mr. Beckford was well versed in prints and etchings, and could detect at once whether it was an original, or a copy; he knew all the private marks of the artists, as well as of the great collectors. His collection of engravings is not only considerable, but consists of the very finest specimens. He gave his mind to it, and whatever he brought his mind to bear upon, it seized with a vastness rarely to be met with—that mind lasted in all its vigour, and suffused itself over a long and active life. His reputation afforded him opportunities, and his wealth enabled him to purchase whatever he considered worthy his choice collection. He frequently regretted to me the breaking up of Sir Thomas Lawrence's collection of drawings, which he considered was the most perfect in the world, and the like to which would never be collected again. He assured me, had they been offered to him, he would have bought them; "but they passed me by, and did not think me worth making the offer to."

He inquired of me what I was engaged upon at the present time, in the painting way. I told him I was making a copy of a portrait of Lady Hamilton—Lord Nelson's Lady Hamilton.

"Lord Nelson's Lady Hamilton?—oh,—or any body else's Lady Hamilton, I suppose, you mean."

"Why," I said, "I imagined her ladyship was even less particular than the Princess Borghese, who sat for Canova, for there were a great many sketches in the Fitzwilliam museum of Lady Hamilton, in a state of nudity, by Romney."

"Oh, than the Princess Borghese, eh?" was the reply; "you must ask the Duke of —— about the Princess Borghese, he can tell you a great deal more about her than I can; but as to poor Lady Hamilton, she was not the most virtuous of women. I was a great favourite of Lord Nelson and of Lady Hamilton. Would you like to see some of their writing?"

"Very much," I replied.

Away he went, and returned with a small letter, one part of which was written by Lord Nelson in a firm character, on the necessity of "*annihilating the French fleets;*" and the other by Lady Hamilton, in making arrangements for a meeting with the author of "Vathek."

As I had been a long time with him, I was about to go, but he made me first run over the house. He took me to a small room, where there was a water-colour drawing of Fonthill Abbey.

"Ah! ah! there's the abbey," he literally exclaimed, pointing to it. I asked him by whom it was painted.

"Turner."

"Turner?" I asked; "he does not paint like that now."

"Oh! gracious God! no! He paints now as if his brains and imagination were mixed up on his palette with soapsuds and lather. One must be born again to understand his pictures."

We went upstairs; pictures, books, valuables were on all sides. We went into his large room, and crossed the arch through the rooms in the other house, down the stairs.

"Well, you must come again. Come when you like—the oftener the better. Believe me, I am sincere—I shall always be glad to see you. Remember me to your father."

He trod upon Tiny; the dog cried, and he took it up in his arms and disappeared. A servant in waiting bowed, opened the door, and I found myself coming out exactly opposite to the door by which I had entered. To my utter amazement, I had been five hours with Mr. Beckford, the greater part of which he had been upon his legs, and had scarcely ceased talking the whole time. This, according to the age he is represented to have died at, was in his seventy-first year. This was the second interview. H.

CONVERSATIONS WITH THE LATE W. BECKFORD, ESQ.

CONTRIBUTED BY VARIOUS FRIENDS.

No. IV.

It was about a month after my first interview with Mr. Beckford, I was returning from a sketching walk, upon one of those joyous sort of days when the air is clear and the sun is bright, when the groves ring with the minstrelsy of birds, and the woods wave gently as if they were nature's fans to cool the atmosphere, and summer clouds come sailing rapidly along, casting their shadows on the scenes below, streaking the landscape with bright lights and shades, that I perceived, a little distance off, advancing towards me on a grayish sort of horse, the author of "Vathek;" behind him was the gardener also riding, but on a horse of a different colour. This gardener's appearance resembled so much that of his master, that he looked like a refracted image of the squire on the air behind. The gardener carried an unbrella and a great-coat. The horse upon which Mr. Beckford rode, was not one of those striking Arab animals, whisking his tail and cocking his ears like Mr. Wyat's pleasant and facetious looking charger in Charing Cross. A common observer would pass it by; but those acquainted with horses would have perceived a peculiarity about it.

"Oh—well—delighted to see you." Such was Mr. Beckford's greeting to me. "How is your good father? How is it you have not been up to see me? You have been to Wick-rocks, quite right, Gainsborough frequently studied there. Oh—oh—what you're looking at the horse—odd creature—Egyptian breed—look, what strange hoofs. Ah, one might suppose it was a descendant from Alborac, and that its pedigree might be found at the *Herald's* office."

He then gave one of his peculiar laughs as if he half believed it himself, and was half enjoying a slight derision at the expense of the prophet. The hoofs and fetlocks were completely those of a mule, but there were no signs of cross in any other part.

"Well," said he, turning to the gardener, "that is our way," pointing to a lane, the gardener had his hand to his hat during the time the squire addressed him, and answered,

"Yes, your honour, that is the way," as if he had been in the habit of saying "yes" all his life (for he was born and bred, gardener at Fonthill) but never "no."

"Well," said Mr. Beckford to me, "come soon, you have not seen half the things." And off he rode, and the gardener after him, as if his Egyptian steed well knew he might have twenty or thirty miles to go that day.

About this time one of Mr. Beckford's servants was so knocked up from the long rides that Mr. Beckford daily took, that he was obliged to exchange his duty, though a strong, middle-aged man. If Mr. Beckford's constitution was not strong, his nervous energy, nervous organization, and nervous fluids must have been "prodigious." He was very much afraid of inflammatory gout, for gout he time after time has told me was in the Beckford family.

Before I got to Bath a heavy shower overtook me, and I was forced to shelter; whilst housed, Mr. Beckford came trotting by, with his great-coat on, and his gardener followed with the umbrella up. Mr. Beckford paid little attention to weather; rain and cold, sunshine and snow, were all alike—he rarely missed his ride, and with the exception of the great-coat, he seldom took precaution against the inclemency of the seasons. The only thing he feared was an east wind—and who does not?

I was with the author of "Vathek," at ten the following morning. The dwarf announced my name, and Mr. Beckford came into the hall to receive me. We ascended the stairs conducting to the upper suite of apartments, he leading, but stopping every now and then to look at some special picture—an oil-painting by Copley Fielding, he directed my attention to, then to a pleasing little bit by Bonnington, the subject of which was two lovers, dressed after the fashion of Paul Veronese, with a couple of greyhounds. The story was not much, but he had made the most of it: colour, touch, arrangement, and neat drawing were all here.

"It's delicately pencilled—poor young man—he died young—he was on the right road," Mr. Beckford observed, in passing.

"The road he's on now, sir," I remarked, "may be a pleasanter one."

"God only knows," was the reply; "he may be sitting by the way-side, begging for mercy, whilst the high and mixed throng of popes and cardinals, and starving poor, happy, are moving on."

There was a full-length portrait of the famous lord mayor—Mr. Beckford's father—painted, I believe, by Hudson, but certainly not by the glowing pencil of Sir Joshua Reynolds, as some superficial observers have asserted. A vigorous, though rather sketchy portrait of the Marquis of Douglass, by Thomas Barker, hung over the door upon entering the drawing-room.

"Ah! there's my grandson," said Mr. Beckford, with all the affection of a most devoted and proud grandfather, "hasn't he a fine head? Barker has not made the most of it—but he has done pretty well."

We passed on into the room, and here commenced the development of the author of "Vathek's" taste. No frittering away with elaborate ornaments—no fantastic twistings and curvings of the tawdry Louis Quatorze style, no heaping of every thing that is costly and expensive, without reference to repose, no pieces of china on the mantel-pieces, looking as if they were going to be crushed by huge masses of bronze beside them; no tables in the centre of the room, crowded with all sorts of curious things under tall glasses, fortune-tellers cut out by young ladies, and dolls dressed up by industrious old spinsters. No, every thing was solemn, chaste, substantial—oak and ebony, marbles and bronzes, pictures and books, gold candlesticks and precious gems. Rich red damasks and dark purple cloths met the eye, but so judiciously arranged, that no one thing drew your attention suddenly; all was calm—every thing was in proportion, plain, yet not monotonous, but happily relieved by graceful carvings where relief was required; a deep repose seemed to reign over all.

Over the mantel-piece in this room hung a full length portrait of the Duchess of Hamilton, by Phillips, R.A. I asked Mr. Beckford if it was like. He replied in the affirmative. The conversation then turned on the fine arts, and I asked him did he prefer Sir Thomas Lawrence's portraits? "No, he's a dandy artist; he paints *à la* Almack's; not but what his pictures of the Pope and John Kemble are very fine. I mean the small picture of John Kemble as Hamlet." "What do you think of his Satan invoking his legions?" "Oh, gracious goodness, that he will go to purgatory for painting it," and Mr. Beckford put on the countenance of Sir Thomas's Satan, flung his hands up in the air, and exclaimed, "Can any thing be more dreadful, or unlike Milton." We both laughed. It was impossible to resist it when Mr. Beckford mimicked any body. There was something so true, but with such a spice of the ridiculous thrown in as to give it a most pleasing relish. Talking about Kemble brought us to the drama, for a hint, however slight, was quite sufficient to make the author of "Vathek" start off, take you to central America, tell you all the discoveries in the regions of Guatemala, touch upon Egypt, and land before him with some strange carving from Italy or gem from Persia, ere you could discover what led to the digression. If he was quick in his actions, his mind was a million times more rapid. Upon the merits of John Kemble, in "Coriolanus," Mr. Beckford spoke in the highest terms; but he became positively enthusiastic in speaking of Mrs. Siddons, her classic postures, her delightful voice, her nice perception, her pathos, and her bursts of passion, were the perfection of acting.

The next painting we looked at was a Sir Joshua Reynolds in his most careful moments. It was a full-length portrait of Lady ——, a member of an illustrious house—treated as a sort of priestess, though dressed in the costume of the last century—a tripod with fire burning on it, stood in one corner of the picture—in the distance a Greek temple, with the glow of evening sunset slightly blushing upon its columns. She was beautiful—English loveliness hung like a sacred veil over her countenance: her beauty consisted not so much in the regularity of her features and nature's exquisite chiseling of their details, as in an expression seized and put upon the canvass to look like life—her eyes appeared as if they had been bathed in the sacred waters of affection, and her cheeks as if a disappointed attachment had robbed them of their roses—could it have been the case? Or, was it but the artist's poetry? O! mighty Reynolds, why has not that academy which you were the parent of, given us offspring more resembling thee?

After looking at the picture, I walked to the end of the room—then to one side, and then to the other, like one that could not see enough of it, and fancies by changing his position he must therefore likewise change the appearance of the picture, during which Mr. Beckford did the same, his eyes riveted on my countenance, and at every step I took eagerly exclaiming, "Ah! ah!" and poking forward his head, as if to provoke some remark. I was silent, and so was he.

To the left of this painting, high up, was the portrait of the Duke of Hamilton when a boy, painted by the same master; his long flowing hair, red velvet coat and collars turned down, gave his grace quite a poetical character; its companion was the author of "Vathek," which has been well engraved by Dean, and published with Mr. Beckford's "Excursions to the Monasteries of Alcobaça and Bathala." Under these were two pictures by Giacomo da Ponte (Bassano), glowing with rich Venetian juiciness and transparency. Mr. Beckferd insisted upon my standing upon one of the damask chairs to look at the one, the subject of which was God sending manna to the murmuring children of Israel. I was horrified. The idea of standing upon one of these chairs, covered with rich damask, appeared to me to be little better than sacrilege. I told him I could see very well. "See—see! to be sure you can see, but not what I want you to see; come, come, get up, and I will give you a hand," and accordingly I was obliged to obey. I am now well convinced that this kind of embarrassing situation was a sort of comedy to him. For, after that, he would frequently force into my hands some most rare or costly thing, such as a piece of Persian enammelling or carving in ivory by Framingo, and bid me take it to the window to look at it. What with my respect for, and desire to please, the author of "Vathek," and my fear a toe or a handle might come off, I invariably felt like a person the first time he is requested to walk a tight-rope; and yet had such a catastrophe occurred, he would have shrugged his shoulders and said, "Well, it can't be helped, every thing will be destroyed some day;" a frequent expression of his.

On the table, in the centre of this room, was the MSS., beautifully illumined, which belonged to Shah Aulum. In point of finish I never saw a missal better got up. There was one other remarkable specimen of furniture in this chamber, it was one of the finest pieces of plate glass, occupying the space where a door once had been; and now, sweet, gentle reader, if perchance of the softer sex you be, say not the author of "Vathek," even in his seclusion, had forgotten the way to please thy sex, for even here a looking-glass was set, so that you—most curious of the curious gazers—who chanced to creep in to see his house on Lansdown-crescent, might your own sweet faces languishingly admire—if there was nothing else worthy your attention.

We now passed from this into the grand room. Tiny, who ever was in attendance upon his master, rose and followed us, and on entering into this apartment, looked up into his master's face, as if to inquire whether there would be time for him to take an additional doze.

"My beautiful Tiny," was all Mr. Beckford said, but it was perfectly comprehended by the dog, for he went and stretched himself down full length upon the Persian rug.

The apartment in which we were now standing, was a long room, well proportioned as to width and height, with a deep red drugget running round the floor—a splendid Persian carpet in the centre, extending itself until it reached the drugget, and there spreading its deep rich purple fringe upon its surface. From the floor, rising to about six feet in height, there was a range of oaken book-cases all round, filled with every kind of work, handsomely bound and of the finest editions—travels, histories, biographies, in every European language, with observations by the author of "Vathek," written at the end in the same language. A little bit of purple cloth, tipped with scarlet geranium, about two inches in depth, was suspended from each shelf, so as to exclude the dust, whilst the ever-subdued colour of the oak was here and there relieved by a little gilding. Above the book-cases, the wall was covered with a silk damask of a red tone, richer and lighter than that of the drugget, and upon this wall was hung portrait after portrait, the likenesses of great and illustrious historical characters, painted by the most eminent old masters, Holbein, Velasquez, Titian, Rembrandt, and Vandyke; then above these was a gold cornice which supported the ceiling, with a slight blush of rouge in it. Opposite the window stood a most costly Florentine table inlaid with various marbles, and which were fashioned into flowers and ornaments. On this table was set a splendid and graceful enamelled vase by Jean Cousin, after designs by Annibal Carracci. On the solid marble chimney-piece of this room, were gold candlesticks, after designs by Holhima, and finally, at the extreme end there was an open doorway, apparently leading somewhere else, but whether to Paradise or to the infernal regions, was upon the first look doubtful, in consequence of the intensely brilliant, and fiery-looking colour which the atmosphere assumed. As this apartment, with its blue, and purple, and scarlet, seemed to be the great hall of literature, and the great tabernacle of learning, we looked more at the books than at the other things surrounding. He pulled down many editions of different works to illustrate his conversation—it really was something extraordinary to see with what facility he would find any particular passage in an author. I asked him if he had a catalogue of his endless collection.

"Oh, gracious goodness! what do I want with a catalogue—I know every book in my possession, and where to put my fingers upon it."

This I afterwards proved to be correct, for I never asked him if he had such or such a work in his possession, but that he instantly went and got it and placed it in my hands. He inquired of me if I was fond of reading.

I told him particularly so, and that I was at that time studying "Burton's Anatomy of Melancholy."

"Strange work," Mr. Beckford replied; "it is filled with deep reading—half your modern works are decanted out of it."

Perceiving a fine copy of "Junius's Letters," I asked him if he thought those forcible productions were from the pen of Lord Chatham.

"Most decidedly not—none of us (for he always spoke of the Pitt family as if he were one of them) ever for a moment thought that they were, and if they had been we should have certainly known it. There is much in them which resembles the peculiarities of Burke, and many of his admirers entertained the opinion so positively, that Burke felt himself called upon solemnly to disclaim the imputation. My opinion is, Dr. Wilmot was the author."

"Dr. Wilmot!" I reiterated, with surprise.

"Ay, Dr. Wilmot; no man had better opportunities; he was a good scholar, a sincere whig, and a most intimate friend of Lord Chatham's. He had opportunities of being fully acquainted with every thing, from his enjoying such an exclusive confidence of George III., which arose from the following singular affair: George III., when Prince George, fell in love with a beautiful quakeress of the name of Hannah Lightfoot. She resided at a linendraper's-shop, at the corner of Market-street, St. James's Market. The name of that linendraper was Wheeler. As the prince could not obtain her affections exactly in the way he most desired, he persuaded Dr. Wilmot to marry them, which he did at Kew Chapel, in 1759—William Pitt, afterwards Lord Chatham, and Ann Taylor, being the parties witnessing; and, for aught I know, that document is still in existence."

"You astonish me."

"Ah, ah,—when you have lived as long in the world as I have, you will cease being astonished at any thing."

How frequently have I had cause to regret that my memory was so poor as only to be enabled to carry away scraps of Mr. Beckford's conversations; for every thing he talked upon was made interesting, either from not being generally known, or from its being instructive by the judicious keenness of his observations. It appeared to me that he elaborately studied every thing, so as to permanently fix in his mind an honest and decided view—that when called upon, he had not, like the generality of mankind, to deliver a judgment which is formed upon the demand of the moment. His opinion was the offspring of reflection. He had the courage to be honest, and his being free from the trammels of personal friendship, enabled him to speak without fear of offending. He has often said severe and reproving things to me, but in such a kind and ingenuous manner, that I felt he truly esteemed me by so doing. If the author of "Vathek" could be chilling and severe, where conceit and folly were conspicuous, his praise could likewise swell into bursts of the sincerest admiration at what was truly good. If he was bitter, it was not from disappointment; and if he was pleased, it was not from prejudice. His mind stood alone, like a splendid firmament, extending over the vast worlds of intellect; but that mind was not to be won by the worship of false idolatry. Woe to him who offered adulation to the author of "Vathek," for sure was his insight into the workings of the heart. To hear him talk of Lord Chatham—the gigantic powers of his mind, and the unbounded goodness of his heart—the true patriotic spirit which he breathed for the poor—the ever wretched poor—would make that Babylon in Parliament-street blush with all its confusion of tongues, and sigh for the days when a Pitt, a Fox, or a Burke rose to legislate, not talk. But the Reform Bill seems to have been a sort of popular besom which has brushed away the remains of their genius, and swept in a parcel of spider-spinners.

I asked Mr. Beckford if he was not returned for Wells and Hinton, and how it was that he did not bring the powers of his mind to bear upon politics.

"It was not my mission," he answered; "I was not destined to lead in politics and was too stiff in the neck to be a follower."

I expressed a regret at his not continuing in parliament.

"Believe me," he said, "I am infinitely happier as I am; besides, the politics of to-day are a sort of Fair Rosamond's labyrinth. I would rather be buried alive in solitude than stung to death by political musquitoes in parliament."

The blazing entrance was now to be passed. Was this the mysterious chamber of the dwarf? or was it an approach to the halls of Eblis. No, it was the apartment over the arch—I had passed through it before, but was not struck with that brilliant flood of crimson light, the cause of which was now apparent. Three rich crimson-silk blinds had been drawn down, so that the sun shining through them tinged the whole atmosphere. On the right were oaken bookcases; to the left, in the centre window, was the marble figure of a sleeping infant, by Roubilliac—but such an infant—such pretty little dimpled hands, and such a pretty little pouting mouth, half open—

that when you looked at it, and saw it slumbering in the bright glow of red which the silk blinds cast upon it, the mind was cheated, and you turned to say, "Hush!" it looked so much like life.

"This is the only son that I was ever blessed with; alas, not to be my heir," said Mr. Beckford. "What think you of him?"

This was said in a tone of voice so calm, so deep, approaching almost to a melancholy key, that I involuntarily answered, "He is beautiful."

"You are right," was Mr. Beckford's reply; "sculpture never went further, even under the hand of a Greek."

In the other two windows were black poppies in vases. From this we entered the bed-room, which was usually occupied by Her Grace the Duchess of Hamilton, when on a visit to her father. Here was a very superior landscape, by John Brueghel, with figures by Rubens, standing on the banks of a most fortunate land, where every out-door flower and hot-house fruit were luxuriantly blooming and ripe at the same moment! A few unpretending oaken cabinets lined with dark purple velvet, and husbanding with modest care gems and rare things of China, were the chief objects of research in this *sacred* boudoir. From thence we proceeded to the front drawing-room of the same house. I might almost say that this room was nothing more nor less than a gallery of Poelemburgs—not but that there were other pictures, and beautiful ones too, judiciously placed, so as to add rather than diminish to the delicate refinements of the soft and enchanting Poelemburg. But Poelemburg, in all his glory, grottoes, caves, landscapes, graceful pieces of architecture, soft clear skies, and fair delightful nymphs, finished like enamels, hang so lightly on the walls, and so irresistibly asking for your admiration, that you could not help giving it. Mr. Beckford, like the immortal Rubens, experienced a singular pleasure in the pictures of Poelemburg, and expressed himself as a most sincere admirer of his beauties.

From the sublime to the beautiful, from the beautiful to the humorous, is a change which few minds can undergo; few intellects are so constituted that the range of their imaginations, and the combinations of their ideas, can extend over such wide fields of differences as the author of "Vathek's." A minute, and Mr. Beckford was all sympathy, and carried away by the enchanting loveliness of Poelemburg. Another minute, and he was chuckling at the excessive drollery of Stothard's Tam O'Shanter, galloping with his mouth wide open, and his eyes staring and looking so dreadfully frightened, and so shockingly drunk,

> Well mounted on his grey mare, Meg,
> A better never lifted leg.

And turning round as he has just gained

> The key-stane o' the brig.

With all the host of "warlocks and witches" pursuing in a dance, and

> Nannie far before the rest.

"There, there," said Mr. Beckford, beating his feet alternately on the floor, "does not that delight you? Oh, is it not deliciously comical, and how it's painted He must have had the spirit of Burns, whispering to his mind as he executed it—it's vastly good, I like it, and so do you."

After laughing and paying due homage to the Scotch bard and British artist, we returned through the same rooms, and only paused to look at the beautiful priestess. We arrived at the front-parlour; Mr. Beckford pointed to a chair on which I sat; Tiny betook himself to the sofa, and Mr. Beckford vanished, and reappeared with an original sketch of a lion, by Rembrandt. I remarked that he seemed particularly fond of animals. He told me he possessed a singular influence over them. To illustrate this, he said, "That when he was in Paris, there was a tigress at the Jardin des Plantes, which took a wonderful fancy to him. Whilst looking at her, the keeper told me that if I wished to please the animal, I would enter the den. I did so," continued Mr. Beckford, and bending himself forward, stared at me in the face, as if he intended me to feel awe-struck, "I did so; and no sooner was I in her den, than she threw herself at my feet, gave a most agreeable growl, opened her mouth with a yawn, and commenced licking my hands whilst I scratched her back. Oh! gracious goodness, she was a very beautiful animal."

Upon my asking him if he did not feel afraid, "Not in the least," said Mr. Beckford, "I felt like Daniel, I had faith, not in my own divine powers, but in the keeper's word—I had almost forgotten all about it, but when Charles X. was at Holyrood, he asked the duchess if I still continued to possess the same influence over animals, and then mentioned to her the story of the tigress."

Our conversation became discursive. We talked upon music. This pupil of Mozart went and sat down and sang, accompanying himself with exquisite taste; no excruciating running up and down and whirling of sounds, as if one note was playing blind-man's-buff with another. It was music, not execution—it was something of the mind and the heart—not of the fingers.

Mr. Beckford afterwards asked me if I had ever read "Vathek." I informed him only the translation, and that but once, therefore I was not in a condition to do it full justice, that it was owing to Lord Byron's admiration that I was first induced to read it. Mr. Beckford then went and brought me the autograph letter from Lord Byron, soliciting a meeting with the author of "Vathek." "Did you not go?" was naturally the question I was compelled to ask. "No," was the reply; but Mr. Beckford's countenance gave signs of an inward regret. "How," I asked, "could you resist such a flattering proposal?" "Oh! to what good could it possibly have led! We should have met in full drill—both talked at the same time—both endeavoured to have been delighted—a correspondence would have been established, the most insufferable and laborious that can be imagined, because the most artificial. Oh, gracious goodness, I have the opportunity of enjoying the best qualities of his mind in his works, what more do I require?"

I entreated Mr. Beckford to give me his opinion of the poet.

"Well, he is a splendid bouquet of intellectual voluptuousness—a genius—a great genius—but an irregular one, his poetic flight is like that of a fire-fly, alternate flashes of light and dark."

We touched upon hours of idleness, *Edinburgh Review*, Lord Jeffrey, and the witty criticism supposed to be written by Lord Brougham. Of Lord Jeffrey he thus expressed himself, "He is a writer of accurate perception, but I do not like these patent intellects of magazines, their writings become biassed—they write too much upon rule, and for party purposes—Jeffrey is too high dried to please me; he wanted a little of Sidney Smith's liquors. But as for Brougham. Oh, ah, eh! he's delightful—charming! so malicious! he is as spiteful as my dwarf—an electric eel. He pokes up his cold nose, electrifies the political waters, and the gudgeons are mesmerised—he ought to be read, he is so clever."

Then turning the stream of conversation, he asked me how the painting got on.

"Not very well—I feel the want of a master," I replied.

"You must have one," he said.

I then related to him how that my father and myself, called upon an old schoolfellow of my father's, Mr. M. A. S., an R.A., to endeavour to take me as a pupil, but he refused, advising my father to send me to the Royal Academy.

"Oh, ah—and to grub out of the trough, whatever hog's wash best suited you—indeed—well?"

"My father did not like the Academy, it was one of the old gentleman's peculiar notions that R.A. stood for Royal Ass. He invariably got angry at the name of any thing Royal. I have seen him thump the table (by way of adding to his argument), until the spoons have rattled against the side of the glasses. 'Don't talk to me,' he would say, 'about Royal Academies—if a young man has talent, that talent will make him an artist without being taught by fifty different masters fifty different manners.'"

"Your father is quite right," Mr. Beckford responded; "I approve of schools, not academies. Well, so Mr. M. A. S. would not take you—why he must have thrust his mind into tights as well as his legs. You must go to Paris."

"Paris," I echoed, "the old gentleman will never hear of it."

"Bring him up to me, I will manage him. You will not like Paris, it is all of a flutter. The French language is delightful, but the French people are detestable; they are a beastly mixture of *eau sucrée* and *eau-de-vie*. Italy will charm you—Florence, the Arno, Valombrosa, with the shades of Dante, Milton, and of Raphael, must touch the tocsin of enthusiasm."

He then spoke of the Italian music, but he was by no means so fervent in its praise. Pasta had been announced to sing at the Bath rooms, positively for that night only, although she sang for three others afterwards; I asked Mr. Beckford if he intended going.

"Oh, gracious Heavens! there is nothing I should like better, but there is only one place which would suit me. Of all the singers, we have never had the like of Pasta—to hear her and Velluti, with his peacockish voice, is the perfection of sounds."

The spot chosen by Mr. Beckford was the best for hearing in the whole room, though only known to be such to a very few. But the author of "Vathek" seemed to know every thing—there was nothing in Bath or in its vicinity, from a hill to a field of moss—from a lord to an intelligent workman, but Mr. Beckford had something to say either in severe condemnation, or in genuine and heartfelt praise.

I contrived to get passed into the room where the concert was to take place, two hours before the doors were opened to the public, and taking possession of the spot which had been pointed out by Mr. Beckford, I sat myself down and stretched myself out into all the pugnacious importance of an American eagle, ready to dispute every inch of ground I had thus monopolized.

I fell fast asleep, and was awoke by, "Oh—oh, oh—ah!" and by Mr.

Farrett, the half-steward, half-secretary of Mr. Beckford gently touching me on the shoulder. I of course instantly rose and resigned my chair to them. Mr. Beckford took the extreme corner of the front row of seats in this sort of nut-shell shape orchestra, but which is only used as such on the Thursday-night assembly. Mr. Beckford by this arrangement, was protected on his right by Mr. Farrett, whilst his person was hid in an angle of the wall. I sat behind. His first remark whilst sitting down, as he looked at the hundreds below, was,

"Gracious God ! what a lot of old women and caps. Now let me have a look at some of your Bath aristocracy—tinsel looks best at night."

This very quaint observation made me excessively uncomfortable, for Lord Somes, a much esteemed friend of my father, was sitting within three of us. I therefore took the liberty of pointing him out to Mr. Beckford. "Oh! well, and that is Lord Somes—the Duke of Sussex of Bath—the perpetual chairman to Bible meetings, ball meetings, gospel meetings, and all sorts of meetings, both sacred and profane." Mr. Beckford chuckled, and I became alarmed lest the remark should be overheard, which only seemed to increase the author of "Vathek's" merriment. The musicians commenced tuning, to Mr. Beckford's horror. "Ah, ah, oh ! I hope they will not keep on long at this sort of work," he said, and his impatience became manifest, which I am certain would have led to his going away, had not Mr. John Loder very soon conducted Madame Pasta to the front of the orchestra.

Mr. Beckford gradually became lulled as the majestic voice of this imperial goddess of song poured forth her pure, chaste, and sublime conception of music, until the whole atmosphere was saturated with harmony. Her first song seemed to have spell-bound the spirit of "Vathek," for he was lost in deep meditation ; this heroic divinity of music, by her voice, seemed to have touched some congenial sentiment, seemed to have whispered to the "old man of the mountain," and to have spoken to him of days long—long passed away, for he suddenly turned and said,

"It was in this room that I first beheld Lady Margaret Gordon, who afterwards became my wife, but that was a good many years ago—cotillons were then the fashion, and the master of the ceremonies used to open the ball with a minuet."

At half-past nine, a message came to say Mr. Beckford's carriage was waiting—he immediately rose and left. I accompanied him to the vestibule, and I wished him good night. On his leaving, he said,

"I shall send my carriage for you and your father to-morrow at two o'clock to see the tower." But, as usual, when he had made up his mind to any thing, he did not allow me a chance of baffling it by saying we were engaged, for he was gone before I had collected my presence of mind to answer his unexpected command. Mr. Beckford's retiring at this early hour was an invariable law he had established for the preservation of his health ; whether at the theatre or elsewhere, he never allowed this regulation to be broken in upon—no matter how interesting or how anxious he might be to gratify his pleasures, these he had taught to be governed by his reason, and to this, as well as his constant out-door exercise, his intellectual occupations, and his apartments being thoroughly ventilated, he attributed that excellent health which enabled him to keep doctors and apothecaries at arm's length.

CONVERSATIONS WITH THE LATE W. BECKFORD, ESQ.

No. V.

It was just five minutes after two o'clock when my father and myself started for Lansdown (in Mr. Beckford's carriage, which had been sent to fetch us) for my father to have a sight of the famous tower and its invaluable treasures. The sun shone brilliantly, but the Victoria Park looked like a deserted shrubbery; nothing was to be seen there, not even a half starved swan escaped from the fire at Prior Park. As we ascended the hill we met one solitary wheel chair, with some disconsolate damsel, half shrivelled by dissipation, and half paralytic by the white and red paint she had been using, looking, *not* like "the last rose of summer," but like the last dew-drop of fashion. As we gradually left behind us the great Finns of the crescents, and the small Fribbles of Milsome-street, looking out for their dinners, Mr. Beckford passed us in full gallop, with his gardener following him. The whole extent of land which now lay to our left was the property of Mr. Beckford, the greater part of which was shut out from the public by pales varying from ten to twelve feet in height. When we had gained the top of the hill the postilion put spurs to the horses, and we dashed by the usual entrance next to the gardener's house, passed through a gateway, under an archway, and were pulled up before the tower where Mr. Beckford was standing on the steps ready to receive us.

After the usual compliments, "Oh, oh: well, so here you are at last,"

I had scarcely carried my eyes from the base of the tower to the top of its lantern, than he again broke silence, addressing my father with " Well, well, what do you think of it, eh ?" My father said he liked it very much, but—" But what?" said Mr. Beckford, without giving the old gentleman time to complete his sentence. Mr. Beckford looked at the old gentleman as if he intended to turn him inside out with a gaze, and the old gentleman looked at Mr. Beckford as if he did not know exactly what he ought to say, and as if he feared that he had already said too much; but Mr. Beckford again asked him what it was he did not like, when the old gentleman told him he did not quite like the uneven masonry of the lower part of the tower.

"Oh," said Mr. Beckford, "it forms a variety to the rest. I only wish the tower had been a few feet higher; the proportions are a little too squat."

"I perceive," said the old gentleman, "you are an able architect."

"I ought to know something about it," said Mr. Beckford, "for I was a pupil of Sir W. Chambers when he was building Somerset House. Had the foundations been stronger I would have carried it up twenty feet higher."

The tower looks like a small Italian villa attached to a campanile, with the lantern of Diogones stuck at the top of it; a lantern not to look after an honest man with, but one to throw a light diffusing the rays of taste into another generation. After Mr. Beckford had been fidgetting some few minutes, expecting me to say something relative to the tower, I at last ventured to tell him that it appeared to me as if the genius of Italian architecture had long been enamoured with the virgin beauties of Greece, and were at last joined and wedded in a happy union by the author of " Vathek." Mr. Beckford smiled and seemed pleased. The chariot and horses were ordered away, it having been arranged that we should walk home through the grounds. We then entered, Mr. Beckford leading the way to the upper suite of rooms. On the landing, and at the foot of the steps leading to the top of the tower, hot air came rushing up through small apertures ingeniously concealed. On this place now stands a tazza of Aberdeen granite, beautifully polished—a great improvement; for, as Mr. Beckford used to say, until he got it, "it always made him feel as if he were looking at a man's jaw with a tooth out —there was a vacancy, a something wanted.

The first door we passed brought us to what was an oratory. A statue of a monk, lit by a subdued light from a small dome vertically over it, and behind which was a scagliola background in imitation of granite, immediately faced us as we entered. To the left and right were oaken book-cases, containing illuminated missals. On one side of the monk was a delightful picture of the Virgin and Child, by Pietro Perugino, on the other St. Jerome in the wilderness, by Mola. Mr. Beckford showed himself in this apartment as much a master of light and shade and effect as Rembrandt was of *chiaro scuro*. I told him so. His reply was that "he had studied light and shade in the Escurial, and effect in the different Roman Catholic churches in Italy." My father asked Mr. Beckford what was his opinion of the Roman Catholic religion, and that of the Protestant. "Why," answered Mr. Beckford, with great energy and earnestness, "the one is the opera and the other the dress rehearsal. Gracious God! the Roman Catholic religion is filled with fine stage effects, glittering crosses, censers, mitres, crosiers, dresses, candles, pictures, banners, processions, perfumes, dolls, and music, from the deep tones of the organ to the delightful squeakings of the pope's eunuchs."

Mr. Beckford screwed up his mouth, and we passed on into the next room, which was the grand apartment on this floor. The same style was discoverable here as at his house on Lansdown Crescent, but more perfected. He had to suit his taste to the house, but the tower was fashioned from first to last under his own directions. From the moment he commenced building it on Lansdown to the hour of his death, he had one great and ultimate object in view.

I soon found my way to a Murillo, the subject of which was St. John asleep, with angels in the background tending his sheep. "Oh, well, I thought you would find that out. I pledge myself that is as pure as a picture direct from an artist's hand can be. No scavengers have been there, eh?" To attempt a description of this painting, with all the sublime peculiarities of the Spanish school, and all the excellencies of this master without any of his peasantish air, is impossible. I only hope that it may some day adorn our National Gallery, where every disciple as well as lover of art may have the opportunity of being moved, nay, inspired, by its holy loveliness and grandeur. Mr. Beckford related the following anecdote concerning the manner in which he became possessed of it.

"When in Spain I saw it in a distinguished prelate's collection. I was anxious to possess it. The pious possessor would listen to no offers. Neither my money nor my entreaties could move him. I returned to England; found a pile of books of a very curious kind in one of my lumber-rooms; took them back with me to Spain, and the holy man could not resist them. We made an exchange. I got the Murillo and he the books. I think the picture worth them, don't you?"

On the opposite side of this room was a very large and fine interior with figures by Palamades. Upon the columns a peculiar effect of light was represented, with the shadow of a window cast as if from out of the picture. This little trick was the delight and admiration of the great majority of visiters who made a pilgrimage to the tower. Few condescended to admire the Murillo. It was one of that sort of clap-traps like Mr. Maclise's ghost of Banquo, which he has introduced into his picture of Macbeth, and which is more ingenious than intellectual, and more calculated to attract the attention of the vulgar than the admiration of the enlightened. Mr. Beckford subsequently removed the Murillo to his house on Lansdown Crescent, principally because the public did not appreciate it. He said, "Had it been the knave of clubs or the ace of spades in a splendid gold frame, it would have pleased them better."

As my father had come simmering with politics, he commenced talking about Catholic emancipation, O'Connell, national debt, Pitt, Cobbett, the Reform Bill, and went over the whole rosary of his favourite topics. Mr. Beckford became as talkative upon the affairs of the nation as the old gentleman himself, and seemed vastly amused in drawing him out. The old gentleman pronounced Mr. O'Connell the pivot of Irish virtue and independence, in fact, that he was every thing. Mr. Beckford said he was a Dan-o-th'-whisp, a terrible *ignis fatuis* riding on the back of the Roman Catholic church, and dancing about in the bogs of Ireland. My father insisted upon his being a great orator, and Mr. Beckford pronounced his orations to be an excellent imitation of arrow-root made out of potato scrapings. The old gentleman vowed the Reform Bill would do no good, and Mr. Beckford declared that it was not only wanted to amuse the people, but might be looked upon as the manufacturing interest cutting its eye-tooth. My father praised Lord John Russell, and Mr. Beckford said that he was a hobbler—that he had maimed himself by a compound fracture of finality, and therefore he always limped after the rest of his party; he was afraid his lordship would dwindle down to a full stop in the House of Commons, for he was only the miniature of a great statesman.

I was all the time looking at a magnificent cabinet of ebony, lapis-lazuli, agates, onyxes, and bronze gilt, designed by Michael Angelo (since removed).

"Ah! ah!" said he, "that is more to your fancy than settling the affairs of the nation—quite right—I always preferred art to politics: they were very anxious to mix me up with them in Portugal, especially the Prince of Brazil, but I managed to slip through their fingers."

There were a few books in this room, and a vast assemblage of some of the most exquisite things brought from the far-famed Fonthill. In the two smaller chambers on this floor, was a most complete and choice collection of the classics, together with some manuscripts. There was a most singular painting in one of these rooms, representing the building of the Tower of Babel, very elaborate and highly finished: but had it not been a tower, it never would have belonged to Mr. Beckford.

We now all three commenced ascending the spiral steps of the tower which led to the top apartment: Mr. Beckford almost ran up; he went with a nimbleness perfectly inconceivable in a man of his age. It was a square room, lit by twelve windows, three on either side; in the centre were the stairs leading to the lantern, boxed up and covered with scarlet.

"Well," he commenced, "what do you think of this for a panoramic scene? Did you think there was such an extensive view in the neighbourhood of Bath?"

"But you may have it spoiled by bad buildings," observed my father.

"Oh, well," Mr. Beckford replied, "in that case I must build and plant so as to shut them out." Then turning to me, he added, "That hill (pointing to one in the Bristol direction) annoys me, its outline is not sufficiently broken; I wanted to buy it, but could not; I should have planted it with trees, so as to have made it look like Rembrandt's famous etching of the three trees."

"But they would have required some time to grow," I said.

"Oh, well, then I must have had some cast iron ones put there until they did, that's all."

My father expressed himself surprised that upon his coming to Bath, he did not give the preference to Prior Park (now the Roman Catholic College on the hill opposite) instead of Lansdown.

"Why they wanted too much for it; I should have liked it very much, it possesses such great capability of being made a very beautiful spot. There was likewise another house near there, which I was in treaty for; but I really believe the proprietor took me for a gold mine, by the way in which he wanted to work my pockets; but you perceive I still continue to wear this little button to secure the pocket, and which fashion the excellent Archbishop of Portugal advised me never to leave off."

After looking at the views (for each window, as it were, formed a picture and a frame of itself), and Mr. Beckford pointing out objects and beauties to admire at a distance which neither mine nor my father's eyes could reach, we descended to the room on the ground-floor. The oaken panelled ceiling, picked out with gold, scarlet, purple, and blue, was rich, effective, and simple. A little circular table stood at the bay-window, formed with a slab of marble from Thibet, supported by a bed and legs of oak, and vigorously chased bronze-gilt. The marble was literally a natural mosaic, incrusted with every variety of hue, and agreeably worked together in every diversity of form; on it stood a china mazarine-purple vase, veined with little blood-red streaks, like darting lightning, and filled with choicest exotics. This particularly caught my fancy: so much so, that I could not help exclaiming, "I wish Mr. Etty or Titian could see this delicious piece of colour."

"Ah! ah! well, I like it vastly too, they are special favourites of mine. I wish Mr. Etty would come; I should be delighted to show him the tower; he is a man of great genius, and the most unpretending genius I ever met."

There was a magnificent Hondecooter in this room—cocks crowing, turkeys spreading their wings, peacocks tossing their heads, chickens running about with their beaks open, white hens with their feathers flying in every direction, and all the butterfly generation fluttering in the air. Whilst I was looking at it, the author of "Vathek" said, "Oh! oh! what's the matter, eh?"

I made no reply, but turned to another part of the room, and looked at a charming smooth landscape by Swanefeld (the hermit of Italy). Mr. Beckford perceived my manœuvre, and insisted upon knowing what I did not like.

"Don't you think it a fine painting?"

"Very," I replied.

"Perhaps you consider it out of character with the room, eh?" And he showed me at once that he knew exactly what was passing in my mind. "Well, you are quite right; but it's an awkward shape to supply the place of. I intend buying another, but it must be exactly the same size and form; no other would suit the room."

He unlocked an oaken cabinet, and placed in my hands a Chinese carving in wood, of an old "Mumpsimus," as he called him, standing and grinning inside a cup. The figure had such a comical expression of face, and was cut with such minute truth, that it was impossible to look at him without being infected with the same feeling of good-humour.

"There, there," said Mr. Beckford, "you have seen Chinese nature, what think you of Chinese art? Oh, oh, isn't he deliciously comical? Why he looks as happy as my Lord Melbourne would do if he were standing in some old dowager's tea-cup."

This made the old gentleman and Mr. Beckford have another round of politics. We now went forth into the grounds; peacocks and beautiful fowls were wandering about upon the luxurious and healthy-looking turf which surrounded the basement of the tower. We passed a thicket of pines and laurestinus; and then turned and beheld the most complete view of the exterior of the tower, looking, not like a petrified spectre, as some German had considered it did a few days before, but rather like the giant tombstone of the sepulchre of Taste. The Bath race-course, with its sunburnt brownish hue, bounded Mr. Beckford's grounds to the north.

"This gives you," said Mr. Beckford, pointing to it, "an excellent idea of the champaign about Rome. You might imagine this dead and solemn land led you to a still more solemn eternity."

The old gardener came with his hoe, his umbrella, and his master's great-coat, to attend us through the gardens. A little further on, and to the right of the thicket of pines, was the spot where, at the hour of the author of "Vathek's" dissolution, was to stand his tomb and that of Tiny's; a gentle foliage of myrtles, laurestinus, and larches, shaded, but did not conceal, these sad emblems of death. Near the tombs were wooden seats, cut out and painted so as to look like Brobdignagian toad-stools. I have often asked Mr. Beckford jokingly, whether they were intended for *l'effroyable Indien* and his dwarf to feed upon.

"God forbid!" he would answer; "they are to tempt Shakspeare's delightful imaginary spirits to come and watch by my side."

Leaving the tombs, and passing under an archway formed of rough and picturesques stones, brought from Wick-rocks, and covered with a delicate and graceful little creeper, which was allowed to grow, and wander, and climb, and to attach its little feelers wherever nature prompted it to do so. We descended some half-dozen steps formed of stones which chisel had not touched, and where mosses and lichens were cheerfully growing and springing up into being, with tints of richest hues. To the left-hand of the garden, the corner was so planted by wood and thickets of evergreens, broken rocks, stumps of trees, with a mustard-yellow colour prevailing, that it instantly brought to your remembrance the pictures of Paul Brill. To the right, pines, larches, bay-trees, myrtles, hollies, and peeping distances, reminded you of Poussin ; beds of dark mould were lying midst pieces of huge stone, with all sorts of creepers, wild flowers, and mosses growing. These fragments of rock not only served to destroy formality, but had a beneficial effect on the more delicate flowers, by sheltering them from the extreme severity of the winds. The walks were pounded spar, so that when the sun shone upon them, you might have imagined that you were walking upon broken diamonds; every step you took presented some pleasing variety of picture, or offered to the botanist some extensive opportunity for information. Passing on to the other right-hand corner, a little spring of water lay still and clear within a basin, tall grasses growing by its sides, with little chirping birds perched on their bending stalks, to dip their wings or quench their summer thirst; clusters of violets peeped out from between the roots of dark spiral cedars, or variegated holly, whilst a gently sloping bank of emerald turf irresistibly made you pause, expecting every moment to see Eve at the fountain, as described by our immortal Milton.

In the centre of this garden was a piece of ground, thickly-fenced round with bushes of evergreens, and which was allotted to the rearing of the more choice and delicate flowers. In the east corner there was a dell, with the appearance of a cavern peeping through large ferns, and overhung with a bolder and Salvator-Rosa-like foliage. By this you suddenly turned, and passed through a thatched summer-house, when a new class of scenery presented itself. We all stopped, and my father broke silence by observing, that he was astonished in perceiving every thing looking so healthy.

"There is nothing wonderful in it," replied Mr. Beckford; "I am persuaded there is a subterranean heat going on underneath. If you remark, my gardener is very careful in keeping off the cold blasts—he is a man of very original mind. Oh, gracious God! give him Windsor, and see what he would make of it!"

But the old gardener shook his head, as if he thought there was no service in the world like that of his old master the squire. The garden through which we had just passed, was surrounded by a high wall, but on the side nearest the road there were two, one within the other, with plantations between them. To our left one of these walls was continued parallel to the road, under which large fragrant bunches of lavender and aromatic herbs were opening their nectaries, and yielding luxuriant sweets to the eager-sipping bee. A long walk extended to about one hundred yards in face of us, at the end of which rose a picturesque house of the Italian school, and in which resided the keeper of the tower, with his wife. It commanded a bird's-eye view of the tower and grounds adjacent, and shut out a most obnoxious looking public-house, with its yellow and pea-green sign dangling at the door. To the right was a most delicious and refreshing piece of grazing ground, perfumed by its clover. Some most beautifully-shaped and handsomely-spotted cows were standing chewing the cud, whilst here and there were sheep reclining under their cast shadows—the Bristol hills in the distance—the river Avon peeping, and the cumulus clouds coming flush to the edge of the hill, made you at once perceive that Mr. Beckford had taken advantage of the scene, and as it were, realised the pictures of Paul Potter and Cuyp.

Before coming through the summer-house, I had observed that the gardener pulled a young sprouting branch, which he kept in his hand. I felt curious to know why he should have done so, and was about asking him, when I perceived a splendid old sheep come running towards us, and one that you might suppose had often stood as a model for Berghem or Karl du Jardin, the wool hung so picturesquely about its head. After receiving the bough (for it was for this favoured animal it had been gathered), we moved on, the old sheep following Mr. Beckford, and Mr. Beckford every now and then stopping to use some endearing term, and to rub its head. Upon asking Mr. Beckford whether it had originally been a pet lamb, he informed us that it had not, but that its taking the fancy for him was entirely gratuitous. The gardener also told me that the old sheep would never allow any other person to approach it. On the walk Mr. Beckford discovered a weed beginning to sprout up.

"Oh, oh, what's that?" said Mr. Beckford to the gardener.

"That, your honour—that—" and the gardener whilst he was saying "that, your honour," hoed it up, and turning round to me, said, "There never was, sir, such a man as the squire. Lord bless you, sir, he not only knows every thing, but sees it—he's the wonder of wonders, that's what he is."

My father and Mr. Beckford, who were a few paces in advance, stopped, and when I joined them, they were both busily employed in settling the affairs of the nation. Mr. Beckford was passing high eulogiums on Lord Grey, Lord Morpeth, and Lord Howick, more especially the latter, whom he pronounced as possessing a mind far beyond the position he had made for himself.

"I only wish," said Mr. Beckford, "he would lead the party. Depend upon it he is the best man for the times; he is high-minded, honest, prudent, and a good man—rare qualities," he continued, turning to me, "in these times for tinkering with the solder of expediency."

"What think you of the Duke of Buckingham?" demanded the old gentleman.

"Why," said Mr. Beckford, "that he is the prize donkey paraded about at all the agricultural shows, and upon which the farmer is seen riding to the Jerusalem of monopoly."

"May I ask," said my father, "your opinion of Lord Palmerston?"

"Decidedly clever," was the reply; "but politics seem to have the same effect upon his mind that opium has upon the brain of a Chinese. He runs after the humming-bird of political chimeras as a Cupid does after a butterfly."

We passed through a grotto arranged into an archway, where crystals were beginning to form, dropping themselves down from the roof, or from the tuberosities of the petrifactions with which the stones were incrusted. Little graceful wild flowers and plants were growing in all directions; on the banks on either side, heaths, with bushy stubbornness, were waving to and fro, and the breezes pressed from the herbs a most gracious perfume. The air, as we went through the grotto, was most delightfully cool, and felt as refreshing to the senses as some iced beverage does to the blood. Upon clearing it, another character of garden presented itself, the lofty walls of which, together with the half-cultivated appearance, might have imposed on you the belief that you were in some garden belonging to one of the convents or monasteries at Rome; the walls resembled so much in colour and structure some of the ancient remains of the old city, and which are still saved and dove-tailed into many modern buildings of catholicism and paganism. My father and Mr. Beckford were still a little in advance; they had got upon religion, and the eminent dissenter, Mr. Jay of Bath. Mr. Beckford spoke most highly of Mr. Jay, both as a spiritual pastor and as a man possessing a very superior class of abilities. This, I know, was sincere; for at the end of a volume of sermons by Mr. Jay, Mr. Beckford has written one of the most pure and fervent criticisms I have ever read in praise of their solemn streams of holiness.

We now came to a door which was unlocked, and passed on to an expanding open space of ground. Some five-and-twenty years ago it was the commencement of the Down, and extensively worked as quarries. It was now the property of Mr. Beckford. Formerly it was a short cut to the race-course, over which you might have seen crowds of people busily pushing on to the festivities of the races. The scene had undergone a change. What had been a neglected waste was planted; the turf which had become brown from neglect and indifference had become fresh and quickened by care—the place which I remembered in my childhood as a spot for idleness, was converted in my manhood to one of the most delightful scenes I can call to mind. If it was not the "happy valley," it was the mountain of happiness—and if Mr. Beckford was not a Rasselas, it was because he was a thoroughly contented and happy man. With a mind the most endowed, a daughter the most devoted, with grand-children the most affectionate ; possessing taste and enjoying health ; having money at his command, and a generous heart to dispose of it; there was very little more required to render the "old man of the mountain" happier, or the author of "Vathek" more content.

Mr. Beckford had so planted this spot, allowing the excavations and caverns to present themselves through breaks in the plantations, that it was with difficulty you could persuade yourself you were in England. "Well," he said, turning and addressing himself to me, "isn't this exactly like Polemburg?"

It was perfectly the character of his landscapes. "There," he continued, "do not those strange mounds appeal to your imagination and suggest to your fancy that they are the remains of Babylon? Oh, gracious goodness," he added, "I do not know whether it would not be quite as satisfactory for those who devote so much time in endeavouring to discover the site of the mighty city, to come here and strive to dig up truffles like pigs."

As we came on the open space Mr. Beckford put on his great-coat, for though the sun still shone with power, there was a slight air stirring. My father observed that he seemed very careful. Mr. Beckford replied, "I enjoy too good health, feel too happy, and am too much pleased with life to have any inclination to throw it away for want of attention. When I am summoned I must go, though I should not mind living another hundred years, and, as far as my health goes at present, I see no reason why I should not."

It was upon this spot that Mr. Beckford, some few years later, caused myself and sister the most joyous laugh I ever experienced in my life, and in which Mr. Beckford himself joined most heartily. His dog, Helena (who was a descendant of poor Tiny's), and whose intelligent countenance had obtained for her the soubriquet of Mrs. Fry, had caught hold of part of a dead rabbit. When Mr. Beckford saw it he cried out, "Oh, Helena, gracious God! Helena, what have you got there?" The gardener said, "Part of a dead rabbit, your honour." "Oh, spit it out; filth, filth, spit it out, you nasty dog." Helena, I say, spit it out," and he stamped and stormed and implored her to "spit it out;" but Helena only dug her teeth in the delicious morsel the more, and turned up her eyes to see to what extremities her master would go. The gardener ran to poke it out with the end of the umbrella. Helena growled—the gardener was afraid to take extreme measures, and Mr. Beckford was obliged to submit to see his favourite dog bolt down this dainty mouthful, to his infinite horror. Knowing the refined mind of Mr. Beckford, and what an outrage this was to his feelings—perceiving his desperate anxiety to prevent the dog's swallowing such filth, and the struggle his kind disposition was obliged to endure lest the animal should be forced—set me off in such a roar that my sister was infected, and Mr. Beckford himself was obliged to join with us; although it was some time before he could forget it, for he continually kept asking "Mrs. Fry" whether she had really swallowed the filth.

Upon this spot all kinds of herbage were allowed to grow, nor was even the humble thistle forbidden from spreading its silken gossamers around. The foregrounds were broken by little bushes of nettles freshly springing forth; foxgloves with their pendant bells, and docks with their large wide curving leaves. No man in his arrangements understood the charm of variety better than the author of "Vathek." He avoided as much as possible repeating himself. If he admired the rarest flower he was not the less insensible to the beauties of the humblest weed; but then he never crowded them. Your mind was never surfeited.

As Prior Park was so conspicuous in the landscape immediately facing us, it was natural that the conversation should in some measure be resumed upon it. My father inquired of Mr. Beckford if he were acquainted with Bishop Baines. "Only by reputation; but I understand he is universally respected by all parties, and that he is one of the most excellent and Christian-hearted men we have about us. It is to be lamented that in these times any of the prelates of the Protestant church should possess the bad taste to be so virulent in the pulpit. There is a reverend archdeacon not very far from me whom I understand is most warlike in his discourses against Catholics and dissenters. Oh, gracious goodness! it must be as painful to listen to this poor mistaken creature endeavouring to spit up hot coppers, as it is to hear my dog straining to get out a sneeze when it's got a cold."

The old gentleman and Mr. Beckford were discussing the merits and demerits of some of the evangelical preachers of the city of Bath, wherein there are not a few, possibly on the same principle that we find a pastry-cook's shop and a druggist's dispensary usually within a few doors of each other. We almost invariably run to extremes; we're either devils or saints; but in Bath some of its inhabitants prefer mixing the two. I left the old gentlemen to finish their discourse upon such divine topics, and, if possible, what was of greater interest to me, the subject of my going abroad. I therefore rambled about with the gardener, seeking out the beauties of the spot, until there were signs of my father taking leave. Mr. Beckford said upon our going, "Well, you must come and see me before you go to Paris." We passed by a side-door into the road; we walked slowly down the remainder of the hill. It was all arranged. Mr. Beckford had said I ought to go, and my father's respect and admiration for his opinion was so great that he did not like to urge a word against it. In a fortnight from that day I went to take my leave of the author of "Vathek." He gave me much kind advice; such as, "to take every thing patiently, to be firm and decided, and to remember that without the love of God no man was good, or could expect to be happy." As he shook hands with me he placed in mine a letter of recommendation to Lord Granville, the English ambassador then at Paris, from his daughter the Duchess of Hamilton.

CONVERSATIONS OF THE LATE W. BECKFORD, ESQ.

WITH VARIOUS FRIENDS.

No. VI.

[It is a striking proof of the extraordinary conversational powers of the late Mr. Beckford, that every body who came in contact with him, seems to have made *notes* of what he said.

We have already been enabled to give specimens of his conversation from two quarters. We have now the pleasure of giving them from a third.—Ed.]

Dec. 16, 1837.—I HAD, some months since, been introduced to Mr. Beckford by, and at the shop of a publisher in the city, where I again met him to-day. He was very chatty, and entered into some particulars with regard to himself which interested me greatly. Among other things I ventured to ask if his establishment at Fonthill was a large one. His answer was, "Enormous! although," he added, "it did not realise the reports which were current as to the magnificence of my mode of living; for instance, I never sat down alone to forty dishes."

I asked him if Fonthill was built upon his own plan.

"No," he said, "I have sins enough to answer for, without having that laid to my charge. Wyatt had an opportunity of raising a splendid monument to his fame, but he missed it." He acknowledged, however, that much of the interior decoration was his own design.

Referring to the fête at Guildhall, on the occasion of the Queen's visit to the city, he remarked that he could have entertained as large a party at Fonthill, in which there was a hall 302 feet long, and 153 feet high. Speaking of his present place, Lansdown, he said that he had more books, and considerably more works of art and of *vertu*, than he had at Fonthill.

I asked his acceptance of a little squib, in Pindaric verse, on the Queen's visit. He took it very graciously, and opening it, his eye fell on an allusion to the giants Gog and Magog—

Fee, fa, fum!

which he pronounced in a voice of thunder, and aided as it was by his gesture, and the flashing of his fierce eye, the effect upon my nerves was almost as startling as if the exclamation had come from the lips of one of the giants themselves. He had, he told me, on the previous day, and at dusk, rode on horseback from Cheapside to Park-lane in twenty minutes—a wonderful feat for so old a man. Judging from appearances, he must be about seventy-five years old; he is remarkably handsome, with an eye full of expression and fire, and in the full possession of all his faculties, reading the smallest and faintest pencil-writing without glasses. His voice, although he has lost several teeth, is remarkably distinct, but his enunciation is somewhat rapid.

Dec. 21, 1837.—Met Mr. Beckford again at my publisher's. His first greeting was, "Ah, sir, your little pink book [it was printed on a fancy paper] has made me laugh finely; and a good laugh in these gloomy days is worth something. It is a delicious poem—[delicious is a favourite epithet with him]—the transitions from scene to scene are most rapid, and admirably managed, and the *dénouement* most cleverly contrived. The action of the little old woman and the equestrians in the civic procession is delightful; although I scarcely think that you will be elected to any of the civic honours on the strength of it."

Engravings from Landseer's picture of "Bolton Abbey," and Wilkie's of the "Maid of Saragossa," were hanging side by side in the publisher's back-room. He spoke in raptures of the first, but condemned the other in no measured terms. Speaking of Collins, who had gone abroad, or was said to be about to go, to pursue his art, Mr. Beckford said, "He had better have staid at home—England will furnish him with better subjects—see what *happened* to Wilkie!" [how expressive the term!] referring to the change which came over the spirit of that painter's dream when he abandoned comedy for tragedy and portrait painting.

He mentioned that he once asked Wyatt if some one—(I forget the party named, but Mr. Beckford said he flourished before my time)—had any taste.

"Yes," was the reply, "a great deal, and all bad."

At our last interview, speaking of Croly, Mr. Beckford said, "Ah! he is a splendid fellow!—the Martin of poetry."

Referring to his place at Lansdown, he stated that he had a terrace which had not its equal in Europe.

A gentleman present remarked that he had heard that Lord Fitzwilliam had given fifteen thousand guineas for a picture—Titian's Venus, I believe—adducing as his authority the curator of the collection. "Don't believe him," replied Mr. Beckford; "housekeepers and curators always exaggerate. I have often received letters from persons inquiring if I really gave such a sum for a picture, naming some preposterous price which my people had attached to it."

Speaking of dumb animals, Mr. Beckford said, "I love all dumb animals." I remarked that his horses looked as if they were well fed. "Ah!" said he in a tone of almost affection, "they are fine creatures!" While on this subject, I may mention that the publisher had a cat which was an especial favourite with Mr. Beckford, who never entered his shop without caressing it. He told me once, that while at Paris he scraped an acquaintance with a lioness, that became so much attached to him, as not only to permit him to enter her den, but exhibited the liveliest signs of satisfaction at his visit. He says he once frightened a lady, who had accompanied him to the menagerie, almost into fits, by relinquishing her arm, and entering the den of his favourite. If there be any reality in the notion that the human eye has an effect on the brute creation, I can readily imagine the subduing influence of such an eye as Mr. Beckford's. It was one on which it was not easy for a human being to look with fixedness.

With reference to the well-known and very cleverly executed picture of the "Pet Lamb," which the butcher is represented as about to carry away from its biped playmates, he remarked, "I cannot bear to look at it —it is painful—I like not such subjects, either in painting or in writing —there are miseries enough in the world without imagining new ones."

I observed that there was, in my opinion, nothing so easy as to harrow the feelings in writing. He agreed with me. Of Victor Hugo he remarked, that he was one of the best of the French writers in his line.

"But," I rejoined, "he writes in wretched taste."

"And worse feeling," was his reply. "There is something about that man's genius which I revolt from—it is—"

"Devilish," I added.

"True," was the rejoinder.

Jan. 26, 1838.—On meeting Mr. Beckford this afternoon, I was agreeably surprised by his presenting to me—and he did so in the kindest and most graceful manner imaginable,—a copy of each of his works—"Italy, Spain, and Portugal," and "Alcobaça and Batalha," in very splendid bindings, with his autograph, "From the Author," on the title-page of each, written in a bold, firm, and clear hand. He alleged, by way, as he would have it, of apology for the gift, that the volumes might furnish me with some hints for a work upon which he knew I was engaged.

Speaking of his residence at Cintra, of which so much has been written and said, he expressed himself very indignant at its having been supposed to be built by himself.

"The fact of the matter," he said, "is this. On my first visit to Portugal, I saw the situation; it was a beautiful Claude-like place, surrounded by a most enchanting country. It belonged to a Mr. De Visme, a merchant, of whom, at the time, I could not obtain it. Afterwards, however, he pulled down the house, and built another in barbarous Gothic. On my return, I rented the place of him; for although he had knocked down the old edifice, he could not level the hills, nor root up the woods. *I* build it!" he exclaimed, "'twas built by a carpenter from Falmouth."

Referring to his habit of taking almost violent exercise, especially on horseback, I asked him if it did not fatigue him.

"Fatigue!" he exclaimed, "I never felt fatigue. I can walk from twenty to thirty miles a day; and I only use my carriage on account of its being convenient to put a picture or a book into it which I happen to purchase in my rambles."

It is, I am told, his custom to go out before breakfast, when resident in Park-lane, and to return with his carriage full of flowers, of which he is very fond. Mr. Beckford at this interview, the conversation happening to turn on poetry, quoted, as a fine specimen of bathos, the line,

Where the foul fungus stiffens.

"That is of the mushroom school of poetry," I remarked.

"Toadstool, toadstool, my dear sir," was his reply.

"He was greatly amused at my quoting, as a sort of set-off against the above, the lines from some burlesque drama of the last century,

Oh, ye with adamantine bosoms, doom'd to know
The iron agonies of copper woe.

1839.—In a conversation with Mr. Beckford I mentioned, with reference to the projected expedition to the Niger, a most absurd suggestion on the part of the originators of the measure, that our vessels should go out unarmed; but that the suggestion was of course resisted, and finally over-ruled by the officers in command of the expedition. Happening to be intimate with one of the commanders, I was in possession of some information on the subject, and was describing to Mr. Beckford the nature of the armament. Alluding to the small arms, Mr. Beckford recommended that they should take some arch-blunderbusses. "There are arch-dukes," he added, "why not arch-blunderbusses?"

April, 1840.—I met Mr. Beckford to-day at the publisher's already alluded to, and had the benefit of his criticism on a portfolio of very fine engravings of the old school, which had been purchased by the worthy bibliopole on speculation. Remarking on a beautiful specimen of French engraving from an old master, Mr. Beckford said, "This is very fine—the perfection of engraving—but differs from the original in that the engraver could not refrain from throwing in a little French taste. A Frenchman always does this: he cannot help it."

On a leaf being turned over which contained some very bad impressions of a rather singular class of subjects, Mr. Beckford exclaimed, "What is the matter here?" There was little in the words, but the manner in which they were uttered spoke volumes. The principal part of the collection was bought in our presence by a gentleman who had no sooner taken his departure than Mr. Beckford inquired who he was; and on being answered that he was a Mr. * * * *, a brewer, he exclaimed, "Well done, brewer! His purchase shows his taste, although he has bought some rubbish with his gems."

Mr. Beckford, from the same collection, purchased an expensive proof on India paper [not laid down] of the Virgin and Child, by Carlo Dolce, I think, and engraved by Raffaele Morghen, about an inch and a half by one inch, for which he gave the enormous sum of three guineas and a half. It was a gem, certainly, and, as regards the impression, probably unique.

Mr. Beckford spoke in high terms of the advance made in the arts by the Scotch painters, instancing Duncan's picture of the entry of Charles Stuart into Edinburgh after the battle of Preston, which I had seen privately exhibited at Mr. Moon's a few days before, and which struck me as one of the finest specimens of modern historical painting I had ever seen. Mr. Beckford added that he had had a very favourable account of the state of the art of painting in Edinburgh from his grandson, the Marquis of Douglas, "A very fine young man," he continued, "with very many noble qualities, and, withal, without a taint of affectation." I remarked that simplicity of character, in man or woman, was the grand charm. "And Douglas," Mr. Beckford rejoined, "has it in perfection; you will see a fine portrait of him by Pickersgill in the exhibition this year."

Mr. Beckford informed me that it was on the recommendation of the marquis that he was induced to read the Ingoldsby Legends, of which Mr. B., expressed himself in terms of high encomium—adding, that they were perfect in their way.

March 29, 1841.—In the course of our conversation to-day the name of George III. was mentioned, of whom Mr. Beckford remarked, that when he *put on the king* he was the personification of dignity. "No man," he added, in his emphatic manner, "could stand before him. I remember," continued Mr. Beckford, during the riots of 1780, Sir George Howard, then" (as I understood him to say,) "commander-in-chief, and who married my aunt, once said to me, 'I am going to the king, who will be pleased to see his friends about him at such a time, and you shall go with me.' Accordingly I accompanied him, and we were admitted to George III. in his closet. 'Well, Sir George,' was his majesty's greeting, as he advanced towards us with a dignity which he well knew how to assume, and which was almost terrific, 'well, Sir George, have you peppered 'em ?' Sir George, who was a fine-looking man, though somewhat pompous withal, replied, 'Your majesty, my regiment has done its duty,' and that particular regiment was very active on the occasion. The king, with one of those transitions from the dignified to the trifling which were common with him, and were, perhaps, symptomatic of that malady under which he finally sank, turned sharply round to me and said, 'Well, I suppose all your chickens are dead,' alluding to the fact of my father, Alderman Beckford, having roofed his house with copper, an experiment which his majesty had on a previous occasion declared would infallibly kill every thing under his roof with verdigris."

Mr. Beckford added that he was introduced at court before he was sixteen, and explained that he owed the partiality of the king to the high favour in which his aunt was held at court. She married Sir George Howard, being at the time a widow and a countess. "For," said Mr. Beckford, "George III. well knew that my father was any thing but amiably disposed towards him."

Mr. Beckford had previously, and more than once, spoken of George III. as possessed of far higher abilities than the world was generally disposed to ascribe to him, and remarked that it often happened that while that monarch appeared to be in the most trifling and careless mood, he was scrutinising with the gravest attention the party whom his apparent trifling had thrown off his guard.

Of Queen Charlotte, Mr. Beckford said that she was very agreeable in her manners, and well informed, but exceedingly plain in person.

The conversation happening to turn upon a young poet, or rather bardling, for he was scarcely fledged, Mr. Beckford said that he well remembered Lady C—— having requested his permission for the young gentleman to walk in his domain at Lansdown, the bard being engaged in the perpetration of an epic, and her ladyship supposed that the solitude and seclusion of the park might aid his inspiration.

"Oh! turn him in by all means," was Mr. Beckford's reply. "And there," added Mr. B. to me, "I used to see him at a distance—for I took care not to cross his path—attitudinizing and smiting his breast and forehead after the most approved fashion."

I congratulated Mr. Beckford on his having so interesting a specimen of zoology as a live poet running wild about his domain, and inquired if he were ever admitted to the tower.

"By no manner of means," was the reply, "I kept him out of doors with the sheep."

Mr. Beckford, in answer to a question on the subject, explained to me that the land was not rich enough for deer.

With reference to Fonthill Abbey, Mr. Beckford once told me that Hayter, the clerk of the works, sent for him while on his death-bed, and told him that he wished to relieve his mind of a burden which had long been heavy upon it. He went on to say that he had recommended the turning of an arch under the tower, but his suggestion was over-ruled, and I believe treated with contempt by the architect. "But," added the dying man, "the tower will make a curtsey one of these days."

His prediction was more than fulfilled: it made, not a curtsey, but a bow—*to the ground*—as all the world knows.

Fonthill Abbey was sold to Mr. John Farquhar for 350,000*l.*, and one of Mr. Farquhar's executors told me, that on the second sale it did not realise more than 150,000*l.*

It is scarcely necessary to mention that the auctioneer on the occasion of the sale of Fonthill was Phillips; who, it was more than surmised—nay, I believe the fact was notorious—had purchased, and in some instances, I am told, imported, articles of curiosity, which were catalogued with those actually belonging to the place. I once casually remarked to Mr. Beckford, that among the things sold, there must have been some *gems*.

"Yes," was Mr. Beckford's reply, "there were; but they were chiefly gems from the *Phillip*pine Islands."

The reader will scarcely need to be reminded of the trick played off upon Gil Blas by the actress, who cajoled him out of his diamond ring in exchange for a counterfeit jewel, which she palmed upon him as being of immense value, and a present from her uncle, the governor of the Philippine Islands.

Mr. Beckford informed me that all, or the principal portion of the really choice specimens of art and *vertu* were removed from Fonthill to Lansdown.

Happening to have in my portfolio two very fine proofs of an engraving by Le Keux, from Martin's drawing in *sepia*, of Marcus Curtius plunging into the gulph, and knowing that Mr. Beckford was curious in the collection of such matters, I sent him one of the impressions; I subjoin a copy of his acknowledgment, on account of the opinion it expresses on that particular production of Martin.

"Mr. Beckford has the pleasure of offering his cordial thanks to Mr. ——, for the beautiful, clear proof of one of the brightest emanations of Martin's genius.

"Park Street, April 15, 1840."

On a subsequent occasion I sent him a copy of a little *jeu d'esprit*, too trifling and ephemeral to be worth naming, but yet of a character which I thought likely to take the fancy of Mr. Beckford, whose sense of the ridiculous was as acute as his perception of the sublime and the beautiful. I quote his letter of acknowledgment:

"Lansdown, Nov. 18, 1840.

"Excellent sport! I enjoy it excessively, and to be induced to laugh at any thing during the present most serious and gloomy times, is no slight benediction.

"Receive, therefore, my dear sir, sincere and hearty thanks from

"Your grateful and obedient servant,

"W. B."

"————, Esq.,
&c. &c."

Mr. Beckford, on several occasions, previously to this, had expressed to me in conversation his apprehension that a serious political crisis was at hand. In fact, I rarely met him that he did not repeat his fears on the subject. On one occasion he informed me, that after a long residence abroad, during which he had heard the most exaggerated description of the disaffection prevailing among the lower orders of the English nation, he returned to England. "But," he said, "when I looked at the cottages, and contrasted their appearance with the dwellings of the peasantry of the country I had quitted, I thought to myself, that these men with their windows so nicely glazed, are not likely to throw stones."

I met Mr. Beckford one day when, referring to a previous meeting at which we each complained of influenza, he asked me how I got rid of mine. I told him I went out to dinner, and was cured by three glasses of Amontillado.

"A pleasant physic!" replied Mr. Beckford. "My remedy was different, but quite as effectual. I got on horseback and rode eighteen miles." His favourite steed was an Egyptian pony, or rather galloway, a gray.

Among his reminiscences of the old French court, he once mentioned to me that while one of a circle in which was Madame Neckar (the mother of Madame de Staël), he was reproved by that lady for a breach of decorum, as she was pleased to call it, in drinking a glass of water without retiring a few paces from the circle. Mr. Beckford hastily bowed an apology, and in so doing, maliciously no doubt, spilled half the water on the dress of the fastidious *arbiter elegantiarum.*

Mr. Beckford, in one of his works, which I will not more particularly name, but the passage is at this moment before me, pays an ironical compliment to a lady, who, taking it for sober earnest, wrote to, and, I believe, called on, Mr. Beckford, to express her grateful sense of the flattering allusion. Mr. Beckford was a hearty laugher, but when relating the circumstance to me he literally roared.

On one occasion, while talking with him in the shop of my publisher, I mentioned a lithographed portrait of Mr. Charles Dickens, then exhibited in all print shops, adding that it was a capital likeness.

"Let us see it," said Mr. Beckford, and it was accordingly sent for. He expressed himself greatly pleased with the cast of countenance, remarking particularly on the small space between the nose and the lip, as indicating intellectual power.

Speaking one day of the power of personation in an actor of the old school,* he said that while on a visit to him, he, unknown to Mr. Beckford, attired himself in a suit of the late alderman's clothes, and suddenly presented himself, assuming the look and air of his deceased parent so admirably, that Mr. Beckford almost believed that his father stood before him. He was, however, I thought, by no means pleased at the experiment.

With reference to the tower at Lansdown, he regretted to me once that it was not forty feet higher. "However," he added, "such as it is, it is a famous landmark for the drunken farmers on their return from market."

W. H. H.

* Garrick, I believe.

INDEX OF NAMES

INDEX OF NAMES